J. E. L. Seneker

(1848 - 1916)

FRONTIER EXPERIENCE

OR

EPISTOLARY
SESQUIPEDALIAN LEXIPHANICISM
FROM THE OCCIDENT

A ✳ BURLESQUE ✳ ON ✳ FUSTIAN

By

✳ J. E. L. SENEKER ✳

To a Ci-devant Condisciple at King College

1906.

Editor's Preface

I grew up in upstate New York, in a small town outside of Rochester. My grandparents on my father's side lived in eastern Tennessee, in Bristol to be exact. This meant that I only saw them once every year or two. Whether they visited us or we visited them, it was always a welcome vacation and family reunion.

My grandfather, Paul E. Stone Sr., was many things: a farmer, a teacher, a principal, a Republican... and a prankster. Whenever we would see him he would stress to my younger brother and me the importance of getting a good education. He would always ask what books we were reading, how we were doing in school, and so on.

So it initially came as no surprise when one year, when I was perhaps seven or eight, he said he had a book he wanted me to "try" to read. I think he even suggested that I demonstrate my reading ability for the family by reading aloud some passages from the book he had in mind. Being a smart, confident young lad I agreed, not knowing that this was one of his pranks.

He looked around for a few minutes, and pulled out a small book that he kept hidden away on one of his overflowing bookshelves. He said it was written by an old Tennessee relative of ours, as though that would make it more interesting. It was wrapped in a plastic bag, and he explained that it was an old book and rather unique and irreplaceable. It was titled "Frontier Experience", but had the strange alternate title "Epistolary Sesquipedalian Lexiphanicism from the Occident". He suggested that I start reading from the beginning of any of the sections, so I think I chose the first Letter. But I couldn't get more than a few words out before I was stumbling and frustrated. This book was like no other I had ever seen, or have come across since.

Frontier Experience or Epistolary Sesquipedalian Lexiphanicism from the Occident was written by J. E. L. Seneker. My grandfather had a copy of this book because we are related to Mr. Seneker. After some research, I've determined that he's my first cousin, five times removed (see the figure below).

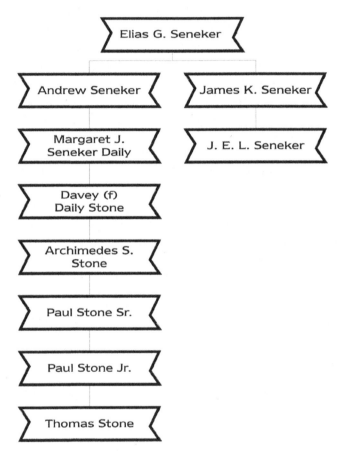

According to the family genealogical records I have, Mr. Seneker was born John Elias Lafayette Seneker on May 3, 1848. His parents were James King Seneker and Elizabeth Bushong, and he had five siblings (James King Seneker had two other marriages, and a total of either nine or ten children).

J.E.L Seneker married Louisa Margaret (Maggie) Dulaney and they had four children: Oliver, Beverly, Estelle, and Lorena. He died in 1916 of empyema, though I do not know the exact date.

Mr. Seneker was apparently most well known as being a long-time Superintendent of schools of Sullivan County, Tennessee, and generally being "prominent" in educational circles in eastern Tennessee. For more on Mr. Seneker and his work in education, see the appendix.

While the individual "Letters" in this book are dated 1872, the book was published in 1906. As this edition is being published in 2008, that makes it the 102nd anniversary edition, a claim that I think Mr. Seneker would have found humorous and worthy of mention on the cover.

The events described in the Letters are not inherently interesting: in fact, Seneker describes rather ordinary locations, objects, and events from the time he spent in the "wild west frontier" of the United States. There might be some interest in the types of things he chooses to discuss, given the different times in which he lived. But what makes this book special is the utterly incredible way that he has written his journal-like entries.

The original text was in a format very much as you will find reproduced here. The original book's physical dimensions were quite small: it measured only 6 inches by 4.5 inches, and the text of the letters numbered only 76 pages. As a result, the exact pagination is different in this edition. However, the format of primary text on the left page and more commonplace synonymous words and phrases on the facing right page, was Mr. Seneker's design. I have attempted to deviate from that format as little as possible. Some oddities of the original text are described in endnotes, while others I have corrected without comment, e.g., minor punctuation, casing, split word, and line numbering issues.

The original text also has a few illustrations, typically at the end of the letters or as ornamentation for titles. Some of these have been reproduced here; others were too difficult to work with. For those that I have used, I have attempted to place them in the same location as Seneker did. One exception is the illustration at the end of Letter III, which in the original text appeared at the end of Letter IV.

I have several reasons for wanting to re-publish this book. For one, I think this book is unique: the deliberately obnoxious, sometimes baffling, and completely frustrating choice of words make it so. I find it to be quite humorous to read for that reason, with many passages leaving me in stitches everytime I come across them. Your laughter-mileage may vary of course.

Further, I have no reason to believe that very many copies of this text were ever produced. But given the rise of publish-on-demand technologies and the Internet, it is now rather easy to breathe new life into works that never had much of a life before.

I'd also like to think that my grandfather (now deceased) would have approved of my reproducing this text as I have here. I hope Mr. Seneker would have approved as well.

Who will enjoy reading or find other use for this book? I'm not sure exactly. Perhaps kids preparing for spelling bees or high school students studying for standardized exams. Those interested in Deadwood-era "wild-west frontier" literature might also find it a curiosity. Perhaps linguists, philologists, American historians, or other academics will find it a curious object of study. Any word-hounds and Scrabble-lovers are also prime readers of this book. And lastly, if you are troubled by the devolution of our language through texting and instant messaging, then this book can serve as an antidote for you.

I really have no idea who will read and enjoy this book, but given an easy means to publish it, I wanted to get it out there and see what happens.

The republishing of this text would not have been possible without the assistance of several people.

My parents, Paul and Cathy Stone, helped with some of the genealogical research during a visit to Tennessee. However, the most aid in this regard came from my Uncle George and Aunt Marcia Stone for not only providing family genealogical information from my grandfather's archives, but also the book *Adventures in Education, 1773-1983* (see the Appendix for excerpts).

As for the republishing of the original text itself, I tried a few different approaches. I set out thinking I could save time by carefully scanning it in and relying on the scanner's OCR software to do a half-decent job of bringing the text into Microsoft Word. This was frustrating, perhaps because I was trying to use my consumer-quality scanner, but I think more because of the nature of the original being scanned: the font is not standard, the typesetting is quite uneven, and it otherwise has little flaws that makes accurate scanning difficult.

I next tried typing in the text by hand, but this was of course quite time-consuming, and so I quickly found myself attending to other projects. I realized that if I was ever going to finish this project, I would need to hire some transcription and editing help. Here is where my colleague Tricia Murphy came to the rescue. As a professional editor, she was able to carefully transcribe this difficult and unique text, and made meticulous notes where there were oddities for me to consider (well, 'oddities' is a relative term, so here I mean potential typographical errors). I very much appreciate her efforts.

As for the book's front and back covers, I wasn't sure what I wanted to do. So I enlisted the help of another colleague, graphic designer Chris Monahan. He proposed several ideas, but in the end I decided to keep it as simple as possible by retaining the original, now quite weather-worn, tan-colored cover design. The only significant deviation from the original front cover, the announcement that this is the "102nd Anniversary Edition" of the text, was Chris' humorous idea. So thanks Chris for helping out with the covers.

I of course would like to thank my wife Susan for her moral support during my work on this project. She agreed early on that the book was a quirky, unique text, and thereby implied I wasn't insane for wanting to get it republished.

And lastly I'd like to thank the folks at Lulu.com for being a great service to help folks like myself get books published quickly and easily. The Internet is a marvel, and the self-publishing industry is one of the many wonders that have arisen as a result.

Thomas Ryan Stone

Table of Contents

Review by Rev. A.J. Brown, D.D.

    "Epistolary Sesquipedalian Lexiphanicism!" Such is the high sounding, pedantic title of a book by J.E.L. Seneker, which was recently placed in my hands. I have never read, or heard of just such a book as this. It is perfectly unique, and occupies a field exclusively its own. The title is characteristic of its style; and gives a clearer and a more correct idea of its character in this respect than anything I could indite. It is made up, from beginning to end, of sesquipedal words; unintelligible, perhaps, to most readers, without the aid of the paraphrastical glossary, thoughtfully appended by the author. The work is a literary curiosity and a puzzle to the common reader; and even to those conversant with the dead languages, from which a very great per cent of the words is derived. To produce this work, certainly required no little labor, philological research, time and patience.

Very respectfully,

A.J.Brown, D.D.
Blountville, Tenn.
Feb. 5, 1890.

Prefatory Remarks by the Author

Horace Greeley's advice to young men, and an inordinate desire to see and to learn something of the world far remote from home, actuated me,- after acquiring all the book lore I then deemed necessary for general purposes, to spend several years in the far west, Mexico, California, British Columbia, Alaska, Ontario, &c., &c. My itinerary grew voluminous as Thucydides. These fustian letters, a few copies of which I have, at the request of many of my friends, printed, give, to a limited extent, that part of my varied experience in Wyoming, Colorado, and New Mexico;- at that time wild west frontiers.

For want of time therefor, I have not arranged them in altogether satisfactory shape; and not being an expert printer and bibliopegist, the mechanical part is not first class. I have greatly amplified the orjginal text, and incorporated many lexiphanic words. The reason for such diction and phraseology is explained in Letter I.

As to evident exaggerations, the reader may decide. There are a few obsolete words, and now and then, a word is used, inadvertently, not exactly in the right connection, yet, the language is certainly English.

There are about 225,000 words in the English language, but only a few thousand are used by most people. How many, for instance, without consulting a dictionary, can make head or tail as to the meaning of the following?:

"I will againbuy the atabal. You are asweved? Yet this is no blushet's bobance, nor am I a cudden, either. Though the atabal is dern, still will I againbuy it."

Plain synonymous words gives the following:- "I will recover the drum. You are amazed? Yet this is no young girl's boasting, nor am I a fool, either. Though the drum is hidden, still will I recover it."

Throughout these letters, not a few words, total strangers to many readers, may be found; but the paraphrastical glossary which I have prepared and conveniently arranged, will enable, even those whose vocabulary is limited, to get the meaning readily and fully.

No one can truly claim to have a liberal English educatlon, and be ignorant of the meaning of the majority of the words in this book. What pleasure or profit may be derived from wandering through this labyrinth, or concatenation of "jaw breakers," competent philological critics may determine.

"La critique est facile, et l'art est difficile."

J.E.L. Seneker
Bristol, Tenn.
Jan. 9, 1906.

Contents

Letter IV
· I attend a political speaking. Minute de-description of the speaker, and a resume of his speech.
· A liberal version of his peroration.
· Fritz, my "chum", gets into trouble. The accusations. Full description of the physical, intellectual, and professional qualities of the attorneys; pro and con.
· The trial, and results.

Letter V
· How I chanced to be at a "big wedding."
· Great preparations. The guests arrive. Description of the guests; how they ate, and how they enjoyed themselves.
· Results of excessive eating and dancing.
· How medically treated, and results.

Letter VI
· Biographical sketch of Fritz.
· He inherits a fortune, and buys a fine cultivated farm. Description of same.
· He falls in love with a western belle, and writes her a letter, making known his love, and outlining qualifications and requisite characteristics his life partner must possess.
· Her reply, giving assurance that his love is reciprocated; but she informs him of certain pecuniary, physical, intellectual, social and moral prerequisites. She also mentions many rights and privileges she reserves for herself.

Letter VII
· I attend preaching. Discordant signing.
· A very vociferous preacher. His appearance, and manner of address.
· Some characteristics of his sermon.
· My trip to the "City of the Plains." A beautiful spring morning. How employed. Plans for the future.

LETTER I
Arenilitic Butte, Occident
November 4, 1872

Most Sophomorical Sir:-

1   Your Græco-Latin epistolet or cabalistical abracabra, lies
2 before me, deciphered and eclaircised to the best of my linguistic,
3 pasigraphical, and exegetical ability. As a merited castigation
4 therefor, and to test your wonted longanimity, I shall recalcitrate
5 by effunding upon you, in epistolic form, my scaturient cornucopia
6 of lexiphanic sesquipedalities, Johnsonian archaisms, exoticisms,
7 neologianisms, patavinities, *et id genus omne.*
8   In former epistolary scribblements, I gave you the
9 concatenation of concomitant circumstances initiatory to my
10 transmigration to this remote section of the occidental portions of
11 our columbian republican coadunation. I have also delineated my
12 periculous adventures among the fucated rubicund autochthons, or
13 aborigines; portrayed various incidents of venations in which I
14 participated, minoratiug gregal aggregations of bison and
15 antilocapræ which abound on the gramineous occiduous plateaus;
16 depicted my primal vision of the illusive phenomenal mirage, and
17 the fata morgana; and in verity, recounted much of my
18 vicissitudinous experience whilst with the caravan traversing the
19 occidental champaigns.
20   I am, however, not oblivious of the fact, that when we
21 imparted mutual valedictory conges, I laid myself under
22 obligations to give you a pantographical delineationof the ponent
23 regions upon which I might cast my ophthalmic organs. As it
24 would be a dilucid evagation from my accustomary routinism to
25 comperendinate the fulfillment of my pollicitations by
26 procrastination or dereliction, I shall, deeming this a suffisance,
27 proemially, or prolegominarily, essay to further exonerate myself

6

sandstone   detached hill   the west

second year at college

1 mystical   meaningless something
2 meaning found   language knowledge
3 writing understood by all   explanatory   punishment
4 patience   kick back
5 pouring out   letter   overflowing full   horn of plenty
6 pretentious words   long words   words out of date   foreign
7 newly coined   local words   and all that sort of thing
8 letter
9 chain   associated   introductory
10 moving across   distant   western
11 American   people governed   union   described in words
12 dangerous   painted red   tawny   natives
13 narrated   huntings
14 making less   herd   collections   buffalo
15 antelope   grassy   western   plains
16 plainly described   first view   deceptive
17 peculiar appearances on the western plains
18 full of changes   traveling company   passing over
19 western plains
20 forgetful
21 give and take   goodbyes
22 full description   western
23 eyes
24 evident   wandering   mechanical regularity
25 delay   promises
26 postponing   omission of duty   enough
27 introductorily   attempt   disburden

7

1 of said obligations, and imprimis, give you a chorographical sketch
2 of this part of our hesperian domain, and a compendiarious
3 enumeration of some of its autochthonal flora and fauna.
4 　　　The superfices of the occidental portion is diversified by
5 many altitudinarian, terrene, lapidarious, and rupellary
6 acroceraunian montanic elevations. Some of cyclopean vastidity,
7 and sublime scabredity. Their mirificant glacious pinnacles tower,
8 apparently above the nubiferous regions, into the caliginous
9 empyrean.
10 　　　The oriental portion is a vast undulating plateau; extremely
11 longitudinal and latitudinous; having few exiguous dingles. Its
12 terreous surface is covered with a most nutritious autochthonous
13 xerophilous graminaceous growth; prinpally, *bouteloua*
14 *oligostachya, bucklœ and tripsicum dactyloides, mesquite, and*
15 *gramma.* This growth sustains equine, bovine, hircine, and ovine
16 quadrupeds in a state of rotund impinguation during the entire
17 hiemal season. Artemisia tridenta, the solisequious helianthus,
18 aculeated cactus opuntia, and multifarious succulent acanthaceous
19 and aciculated cactaceous plantage, and floriferous, herbaceous,
20 and graminifolious garniture luxuriate in many localities.
21 　　　The fluvial meanders are limited, and originate from the
22 liquefaction of the vast niveous and glacial accumulations in the
23 montanic regions. None are navigerous, but they are truttaceous
24 and anatiferous. Some are, pactolian, and all are extremely
25 relucent, and possess a great degree of diaphaneity. None tardy in
26 profluence. At many points, their rivages, especially in the vicinity
27 of the embouchures, or disemboguements of arroyos, are replete
28 with a promiscuity of asperfolious, bacciferous, or cocciferous,
29 vinaceous arundinaceous, and other bushments.
30 　　　Myriads of venene, umbelliferous, corymbiferous,
31 racemiferous, urticaceous, fructiferous, anthophorous, or
32 floriferous plantage, and multifarious spontaneous esculent
33 products also abound. The autochthonous arboreous growth
34 consists of acerose sempervirent and perdifolious silva, and
35 boscages. By no means, ofimmane arduity, or totally devoid of

1 In the first place   local description
2 western   brief
3 detailed account   native   animal and vegetable life
4 face   western   varied
5 lofty   earthy   rocky   cliffy
6 thunder smitten   mountains   gigantic   immensity
7 rugged   glittering   icy   peaks
8 cloud bearing   dark
9 highest heavens
10 eastern   wavy   highland
11 long   wide   narrow   valleys
12 earthy   native
13 drouth resisting   grass kind
14 native grasses on the western plains
15 horses, cattle, goats, sheep
16 round   fatness
17 winter   sagebrush   sunflowers
18 prickly pear   various kinds   juicy   thorny
19 spiny   cactus   flower bearing   herb kind
20 grass leaved   grow abundantly
21 rivers
22 melting   snow   icy
23 mountains   boat bearing   full of trout
24 duck bearing   noted for golden sands
25 glittering   transparency
26 onward flow   banks
27 outlets   small streams   filled
28 general mixture   rough leaved   berry bearing
29 vine kind   reed kind
30 poisonous   umbel   corymb
31 raceme bearing   nettles   fruit bearing
32 flower bearing   various kinds   uncultivated   eatable
33 native   tree
34 needle leaf   leaf-evergreen   leaf shedding   forests
35 groves   great-height   without

1 aduncities, nodosities and knags. Disboscation by succision and
2 conflagrations will deplete same in the next decade.
3   The reptatory, pennigerous, bisulcous and unguiculated
4 feral entities of this domain are; ousels, ptarmigans, ortolans,
5 leverocks, trochidæ, shelducks, cryals, kokobs, creeples,
6 crotaluses, carcajous, logomyes, castors, marmots, malodorous
7 mariputs, *spilogale putorius, lepus campestris, oves montanæ*,
8 *antilocapræ*, bison, spermophiles, coyotes, grizzlies-ursus
9 horribilis, and other animals of the murine, sciurine, feline, canine,
10 leporine, vulpine, lupine, ursine, cervine, caprine, ovine, and
11 equine genus. Also, pennipotent accipitrine and aquiline raptors.
12 There are apparently interminable areas almost wholly
13 monopolized by the *cynomys ludovicianus*. Viewing the ludicrous
14 antics of these lusory sciurine burrowing rodents, in their
15 circumcursations, or perched, *a la homo* upon the apices of their
16 coniform tumulosities incessitously allatrating, one cannot control
17 his risibles.
18   The intermontane sections of this region are as auriferous
19 and argentiferous as any of the austral, remote austrine occidental,
20 or extreme occidental and septentrional sections of this republican
21 adunation. They are also ferrifeous carboniferous, or
22 anthraciferous, plumbiferous, and cupriferous.
23   The uberty, or fecundity of the soil in the battable sections,
24 when properly stercorated and irrigated, exuperates enarration.
25 Besides frumentarious products - which yield a most siliginose
26 flour - there are produced in campestrian and olitory enclosures;
27 brank, citruls, sarmentaceous fragaria cucurbitaceous, acetarious,
28 fabaceous, and, in verity, multifarious oleraceous edibles.
29   There are vast arid alkaligenous areas, and arenarious
30 agerations, multitudinous conglomerate buttes, and
31 circumdenudated arenilitic elevations. Such areas not being
32 scaturiginous, and arable, will ever be sparcely[1] populated.
33   The nummulary majoration, or crescive ditation of the terre
34 tenants originates from agistment, coemption and vendition of
35 equine, bovine, and lanigerous ovine quadrupeds, or rotherbeasts
36 from attention to geoponics, or agronomy; from usurarious

1 crookedness knots broken limbs forest clearing cutting down
2 great fires   exhaust   ten years
3 creeping   feathered   cloven footed   claw footed
4 wild   beings   blackbirds   partridges   small birds
5 larks-humming birds-wild ducks-herons-poisonous-snakes-reptiles
6 rattlesnakes-badgers-hares-beavers-woodchucks-bad smelling
7 polecats   jack rabbits   mountain sheep
8 antelope   buffalo   squirrels   prairie wolves   grizzly bears
9 mouse-squirrel-cat-dog
10 hare-fox-wolfe-bear-stag-goat-sheep
11 horse   kind   strong winged   hawk   eagle   birds of prey
12 unlimited
13 in full control   prairie dogs   laughable
14 playful   squirrel like   gnawers
15 running around   like a person   tops
16 hillocks   continuously   barking
17 inclination to laugh   gelastic muscles
18 between mountains   gold and silver bearing
19 south-distant
20 south-western   western-northern
21 union   iron bearing
22 coal-lead bearing   copper bearing
23 fertility   tillable
24 manure   watered   exceeds   description
25 grain   excellent
26 field   garden
27 buckwheat   melons   strawberries   squashes   salad plants
28 beans   many kinds   pot herbs   eatables
29 dry   alkaline   sand
30 heaps   many   mixed rock   detached hills
31 weather worn   sandstone
32 abounding in springs   tillable
33 money   increase   growing rich
34 inhabitants   cattle grazing   buying-selling-horses-cattle
35 wool bearing sheep   black cattle
36 farming   high interest

1 contracts and usufructuary holdings; from enhancement in value of
2 preempted terra firma; from venations, agiotage, mining,
3 emporetical pursuits, or mercature, and from general negotiations.
4   The paucity of population in some localities possesses a
5 consimilitude to a mere exiguity.
6   The life of many is bucolic and nomadic. The oppidan, and
7 many villatic communities the optimity of society prevails.
8 However, the cordial compagination of so heterogeneous a mass,
9 and farraginous concurrence of all nationalities, as is the case in
10 some localities, demands time. There must be a prior detruncation
11 of the truculence and inurbanity of some of its divisions to obtain
12 the optimity of society and secundation. Appetition for aucupation,
13 cynegetics, alectryomachy, tauromachy, and circumforaneous
14 evagations, must undergo imminution. The comportance of the
15 major portion of the occidental leod is, by no means, truculent,
16 scelestic, or immorigerous, nevertheless, many are subdolous, and
17 have a great inhiation for captation, feneration, the coacervation of
18 pelf, preemption and coemption of terra firma, and participating in
19 festal jovialities.
20   The ethics of many are greatly maculated by the vendition
21 and bibacity of aqua vitæ. Localities replete with cades of
22 aguardienta, pupelo, skink and bub, are patrocinated by, and
23 thronged with bibbers, whose comates, condisciples and
24 compotators are dolts, fanfarons, jobbernowls, anserous
25 nincompoops, maudlin gaberlunzies, temulent wantwits,
26 linguacious borachios, and bateful barrators.
27   They sometimes initiate their saturnalian revelries with
28 xerophagy, and the manducation of ragouts, saveloy, and polony,
29 to give an acumen to their gusto for the imbibition of inebriating
30 potations. As a sequence, what stultiloquence! What random
31 tentations at the enodation of some vulgar enigma! What
32 perpotation and ruinous ebriety! What mutual pugnacity issuing in
33 testy concertations and sanguinary pugilisms! Such rendezvous are
34 terrestrial pandemoniums.
35   Relative to myself; as you are cognizant, for some time
36 subsequent to my discession from home, I sojourned with

1 use without pay   increase
2 entered   land   hunting   stockjobbing
3 merchandizing   trading
4 scarcity
5 similarity   scantiness
6 herding   roving   town
7 village   best state
8 genial   uniting   unlike
9 mixed   collection
10 cutting off
11 savageness   incivility
12 best state   prosperity   desire   birdcatching
13 hunting with dogs   cockfighting   bullfighting   roundabout
14 roving   decrease   behavior
15 western   people   savage
16 wicked   rude   crafty
17 desire   catching favor   money interest   heaping
18 money   entering   buying up   land   taking part
19 feasting   merriment
20 morals   stained   selling
21 drinking   strong intoxicants   filled   kegs
22 brandy   whisky   ale   beer   patronized
23 drinkers   associates   fellow students   co-drinkers
24 blockheads   bullies   ignorant fellows   gawky simpletons
25 tipsy sponges   drunken halfwits
26 talkative drunkards   contentious   encouragers of lawsuits
27 begin   noisy jollity
28 eating dry meat   chewing   highly seasoned hash   dry sausage
29 keenness   appetite   drinking   intoxicating
30 draughts   result   foolishness
31 guessing attempts   explanation   riddle
32 excessive drinking   drunkenness   give and take   fisticuffs
33 crabbed disputes   bloody   knockdowns   resorts
34 earthly   council chambers of the demons
35 aware
36 after   departure

1 agnations and cognations, who are amnicolists and engaged in
2 terraculture, or agricolation. The circumambient and circumjacent
3 country is interamnian, nemorous aud paludal, or palustral. My
4 vocation was at first, subtegulaneous and sedentary, but
5 subsequently became wholly extraforaneous. Prior to becoming
6 inured to a castrensial mode of life, I very injudiciously submitted
7 to humicubations during pernoctations; which during the initial
8 part of my castrametations, and alfresco employment, in
9 connection with nocturnal irrorations, miasmatic exhalations, and
10 the dankishness of the atmosphere, generated by a want of apricity,
11 were extremely febrifacient; causing tertiary quassation and
12 febriculosity. Infrigidation, formication, cardialgy, allotriophagy
13 and wamble, succeed by calenture, found introgression into my
14 corporeal organization. I was, medicamentally adjuvated by a
15 rurigenous charlatanical anencephalous medicaster, who, not being
16 extra scient in acology, iamatology, soteriology,
17 pharmacodynamics and in the impartation of eccritics ecphractics,
18 and other pharmacons, and moreover, having erroneously
19 diagnosticated my case, greatly minorated my eupepsy, and
20 occasioned me to spend many insomnious nights.
21   In my brief swevens I endured circumvolation of
22 pigwidgeons, cacodemons, and odible simulachres in my harns.
23 Upon these supervened cynorexia, leucophlegmacy, turgid muns,
24 and cinchonism. I am now robust physically and sane mentally, or,
25 *mens sana in corpora sano*, with the exception of a slight
26 odontalgia and cephalalgia, but not the slightest symptom of
27 nostalgia. Eulogium to the supermundane powers for the
28 revivification of my physical organization, and for my
29 invalescence and complete analepsis by means of pyretics,
30 cholagogics, peptics, anticausotics, and other medicamenta; also,
31 balneotherapy, kinesipathy, or kinesiatrics, and migration to this
32 salubrious clime.
33   Since my ubication here, my functions have been
34 bibliopolistical, bucolical, agronomical, paideutical, or
35 pedagogical, and negotiatory. I have prererrated the ponent regions

1 relatives   kinsfolk   living near rivers
2 farming   surrounding   adjoining
3 between rivers   timbered   marshy
4 indoors   sitting
5 afterwards   outdoors
6 before   accustomed   camping   unwisely
7 lying on the ground   night watches   first
8 camping out   outdoor
9 nightly   dews   poisonous vapors
10 dampness   sunshine
11 fever producing   every third day chills
12 fever chilliness creeping-sensation heartburn depraved-appetite
13 sick stomach   high fever   entrance
14 body   with medicine   treated
15 countryborn   pretentious   brainless   quack
16 versed   science of medicine   of remedies   of health
17 effects of medicine   giving   emetics   purgatives
18 drugs
19 recognized ailment from symptoms   lessened   good digestion
20 sleepless
21 dreams   flying around
22 fairies   evil spirits   horrible   ghosts   brain
23 followed   dog like appetite   cold sweats   swollen mouth
24 quinine deafness   stout   sound in mind
25 sound mind in sound body
26 toothache   headache
27 homesickness   great praise   above the world
28 restoration
29 getting well   recovery   fever medicine
30 liver medicine   digestives   fever remedies   medicine
31 bath cure   movement cure   moving
32 healthful
33 being present   duties
34 bookselling   herding   farming   teaching
35 trading   traveled over   western

quite extensively, and have witnessed many peregrinities, and neoteric occurrences.

I will now terminate this protracted autoschediastical scribblement by imparting to you the verity, that as yet, feminality has not parlously effascinated me, though I am not by any means, a misogynist or a misogamist; affected with neither gyneolatry or gynephobia; though somewhat of a philogynist. Desiderating not to be gyved with connubial relations, I have come to the illation to be the solivagant yet many annuary epochs.

I shall offer no exculpation for hieroglyphical chirography, autoschediastical orthology, cacography and cacology; but leaving it to your to decipher, etymologize, and eclaircise, to the best of your lexigraphical, lexicological, orismologica, and philological ability. I am,

Most lexiphanically,

Your quondam condisciple,

Ivan

1 strange things
2 novel happenings
3 end   careless
4 writing   fact   woman kind
5 dangerously   charmed
6 marriage or woman hater   woman worship
7 woman dread   woman admirer   desiring
8 fettered   marriage   conclusion
9 lone wanderer   years
10 excuse   difficult to read   hand writing
11 careless   description   scrawling   bad choice of words
12 make out the meaning   find origin   explain
13 word defining   knowledge of use of words   knowledge
14 of technical terms and language laws
15 dictionary affected
16 former   fellow student

LETTER II
Mirage Plateau, Occident
Dec. 3, 1872

Most Automathic and Glottological Sir:

1   In my prevenient catachrestical epistolographical
2   missile, I essayed to portray to you the chorography of this
3   portion of the ponent regions. My present elucubration
4   shall be narratory of incidents in my chequred² experience
5   here.
6   The caravan with which I traversed the occidental
7   plateau, reached its destination during the canicular days.
8   Here, subsequent to the tarriance of several hebdomads,
9   having an appetency to perlustrate the Hesperian domain
10   still further, I entered into a pactitious agreement as
11   peripatetic itinerant bibliopole.
12   This was quite consentaneous with my nature; for,
13   as you know, from my earliest juvenility, I have been an
14   ardent bibliophilist.
15   Receiving a compendiarious prospectus, I prolated
16   valedictions to my *compagnos de voyage* and inchoated
17   solvagant perambulations.
18   I now realized the fact that I was in a peregrine
19   land, unkent, a fren, a peripatetic pedestrious viator, and
20   apparently isolated, with the salvo of a canine quadruped,
21   whose mordacious, latrant, lusorious, and venatic qualities
22   are without parity. Cicurated and divested of his
23   acharnement and curstness, he has been of great utility to
24   me in his indagation of game in their latitations,
25   latilbulums, or hibernaculums; and for his pervigilations.
26   By his cerberean latrations, he has kept in abeyance the

Deceptive appearance   high plain   west

self taught   language knowing

1 former   farfetched   letter
2 tried   describe   local geography
3 western   lamplight composition
4 giving particulars   changeful
5
6 company of movers   passed over   western
7 high plain   dog days
8 delay   weeks
9 desire   look at closely   western
10 contract
11 traveling   walking   book agent
12 in accord
13 youth
14 passionate   book lover
15 concise   summary   pronounced
16 goodbyes   fellow travelers   began
17 lonely   inspective walking
18 strange
19 unknown   stranger   walking   traveler
20 alone   exception   dog
21 biting   barking   playful   hunting
22 equal quality   tamed
23 fierceness   crabbedness
24 searching out   hiding places
25 dens   winter homes   watchfulness
26 loud mouthed   barking   check

whole noctivagant furacious race; especially, during the
nocturnal hours.

I onerated my dorsal part with a portmanteau for the
vectitation of my habiliments. My humeral, or acromial
projecture, I also onerated with an instrument consisting of
a ligneous stock and ferreous tube, for the enecation of
aligerous and volant bipeds, and those animals that are
given to latrociny, or a predacious life.

With this armature and accoutrements, I took up my
line of march in a septentrio-occidental direction, for
distant oppidan and villatic communities. Amplifying
claritude occupied the argent fields above; human, belluine,
and other entities sustained the radiating caloric of Phœbus.
Exhilarating euphony seemed to possess entire ubiquity.
Under this buoyant physical revivification I transcended
acclivities and declivities, until the rayonant solar luminary
had attained meridional arduity, pouring down upon me his
calefactory radiations; so that my corporeal organization
was, in totality, subjected to redundant sudations,
necessitating me to bring my bombycinous sudary into
frequent requisition. After having participated in a
collation, I submitted my corporeity to quiescence in a
resupine position; which proved very acopic, and
effectuated an instauration of my physical energies. Having
indulged in something like pandiculation, at least, a sort of
involuntary calisthenical exercise, I resumed the elongation
of my pedaneous locomotion, and protracted it till past
crepuscule. Thus ended my primal days itineration, varied
by a multiplicity of peregrinities and neoteric occurrences.
But oh! My defatigation, and the turgescence of my
pedalian extremities! The cataphracted epiderdermal
integument abraded from my malleolar processes and
calcaneal protrusions. My sinistral tendo-achilles and the
dorsal part of my dextral hallux extensively vesicated and
excoriated. But you know, the initial part of all enterprises
is arduous.

1 night roving   thievish
2 night
3 burdened   back   leather bag
4 carrying   clothes   shoulder   shoulder
5 burdened
6 wooden   iron   killing
7 winged   flying   two footed animals
8 robbery   preying
9 protective outfit   equipments
10 north western
11 towns and villages   increasing
12 brightness   silvery   beasts
13 beings   sending out   heat   the sun
14 cheering   harmony   everywhere
15 uplifting   passed over
16 uphills   downhills   beaming   sun
17 noon   height
18 heating   rays   body
19 completely   excessive   perspiration
20 silken   handkerchief
21 use
22 cold luncheon   body   rest
23 prostrate   relieving weariness
24 brought about   restoration
25 drowsily stretching
26 bodily exercise
27 walking   movement
28 twilight   first   walking
29 great many   strange things   novel   happenings
30 weariness   swollen state
31 feet   hardening   outer skin
32 covering   rubbed off   ankles   heels
33 left   heel tendon
34 back part   right   big toe   blistered
35 skinned   beginning
36 laborious

1   Subsequently to a very sumptuous vespertine repast,
2 I intimated to the caterer for human and belluine animality
3 that, feeling quite superlatively elumbated, and being
4 somewhat somniculous, I was propense to an early
5 couchee; and requested that he indigitate to me a cubicular
6 department, or dormitory, in which I might enjoy
7 somniferous quietude. I elicited from my host an
8 obstriction to cause my experrection when the caligation of
9 the night was yielding to the clarity of the remeant exortive
10 solar sphere. Prior to decumbency on my couch, I
11 submitted my pedal and crural organs to a defecation by a
12 copious lavation with medicated saponaceous abstergents.
13 This pediluvy and ablution, though I yet suffered a slight
14 vellication in my femoral organs, gave me a proclivity for
15 an indulgence of my somnolency without intercission. In
16 the matin, according to paction, the aubergist exsuscitated
17 me at the first canorous peal of the chanticleer. After the
18 customary matutinal mannal and facial ablution and
19 abstersion, and capital pectination, and a very satisfactory
20 impletion of my epigastric receptacle, I asked for a
21 supputation with him; and having duly adjusted the same, I
22 resumed my ambulatory incession. The ceruleous canopy
23 was merging into fulgidity from the ascending rayonant
24 Phæbus. Every entity about me seemed to revel in universal
25 resuscitation. I performed my quotidian locomotion for
26 several diurnal revolutions; witnessing a multiplicity of
27 occurrences homologous to those already specified.
28   One day, when the solar sphere had culminated, I,
29 being much exantlated from continuous deambulation, gave
30 way to a recubation under an isolated, multiramous,
31 umbrageous tree, attiguous to the trail, for the purpose of
32 exercising my masticators upon the contents of my
33 viaticam. Having furnished refocillation to my system,
34 recumbent on my dorsal part, I viewed the plumous tenants
35 of the air in their evolutions among the ramifications of the
36 tree, and the illusive mirage in the distance. Having

1 after   evening
2 host   beast
3 extremely   wearied
4 sleepy   inclined
5 bedtime   point out
6 bed room   sleeping apartment
7 sleep producing
8 obligation   awakening   darkness
9 brightness   returning   rising
10 sun   lying down
11 feet   legs   cleansing
12 abundant   washing   soap   cleansers
13 foot baths   bathing
14 twitching   thighs   inclination
15 drowsiness   interruption
16 morning   agreement   host   aroused
17 musical crowing   rooster
18 morning   hand   face   washing
19 wiping clean   head   combing
20 filling   stomach
21 settlement
22 walking   progress   blue   sky
23 brightness   rising   beaming
24 sun   being
25 cheerfulness   daily   marches
26 daily   rounds   great many
27 happenings   similar   mentioned
28 sun   reaching highest point
29 exhausted   walking
30 sitting down   solitary   many branches
31 shady   near   road
32 teeth
33 provision bag   refreshment
34 lying   back   feathered   occupants
35 flying around   branches
36 deceptive   peculiar appearance

1 discalceated, I perfricated my recrudescent and attrited
2 pedal organs with an iatroleptical cerate, and then,
3 becoming profligated with somnolency, I soon relapsed
4 into a post prandial siesta. Schnell, for that was the
5 cognomination of my canine companion and presidiary, –
6 advigilated. I was, however, soon suscitated by an electrical
7 detonation from the septentrional part of the horizon. So
8 soon as my ophthalmic organs had undergone patefaction, I
9 realized that nubiferous gales were in operation,
10 agglomerating a most ominous and impendent
11 cumucirrostratus thunderhead. The welkin was rapidly
12 obnubilating, and tenebrosity amplifying. The
13 crispisulcations and furcations of the fulgurations became
14 vivid, and the fulminations horrisonous. In a brevity of time
15 there was a copious precipitation of pluvious globules,
16 which subjected me and Schnell to thorough madefaction.
17 The arroyos assumed such ampliations as might be instyled
18 a local torrential cataclysm. Aqueous domination prevailed
19 on earth; igneous puissance and fulmineous reverberations
20 predominated in the nubiferous regions; and a resistless
21 ventosity maintained horrendous boations in the
22 atmosphere. The fulgurations communicated their igneous
23 potency to a rancho sans paratonnerres, setting in it
24 flagration; terminating in entire incineration. Being
25 untenanted, no one fell a prey to cremation. I and Schnell
26 had to engage in the transilience and tranation of several
27 arroyos; which greatly augmented the ponderosity of our
28 envelopes. Ultimately, as the day began to advesperate, but
29 prior to the cadence of Phœbus,-with pedal envelopes and
30 the inferior portion of my femoral habiliments subjected to
31 quite an illutation, – I arrived at an adobe chalet.
32 Anthracitic and ligneous combustibles were deposited in a
33 spacious calefactor, and accended with an allumette, giving
34 me an opportunity for torrefaction, or divaporation. I was
35 soon summoned to the refectory by tintinnabular
36 reverberations, where I found ample cenatory refreshments.

1 removed shoes   rubbed over   grown sore again   skinned
2 feet   medicated   salve
3 overcome   drowsiness   fell into
4 after dinner nap
5 name   dog   guard
6 watched   aroused   thunder clap
7 northern
8 eyes   opening
9 cloud bearing
10 rolling up   threatening
11 rain storm cloud   visible sky
12 becoming clouded   darkness   increasing
13 zigzagedness   forkings   lightnings
14 blinding   thunder   horrid sounding   shortness
15 abundant   downpour   rain   drops
16 soaking
17 water courses   dimensions   called
18 rushing flood   water   ruling
19 fiery   power   thunder   echoes
20 held full sway   cloud bearing
21 wind storm   horrid   roarings
22 lightning   fiery
23 power   cabin   lacking   lightning rods
24 flames   reduction to ashes
25 unoccupied   burning human bodies
26 leaping and swimming across
27 water courses   increased   weight
28 coverings   grow late
29 going down   sun   foot   coverings
30 pants
31 mud bath   mud brick   herdsman's hut
32 coal   wood   fuel
33 large stove   kindled   friction match
34 warm and dry
35 dining room   bell ringing
36 echoes   supper

1 Tenebrosity having by this time encircled our moiety of
2 this mundane sphere, I soon sank into the gremium of
3 Morpheus.
4   The day subsequent to the procellous vesper on
5 which I effectuated the arefaction, or calefaction of my
6 habiliments was not very inservient to the progress of a
7 pedestrious viator. It is true, the atmospheric regions, at
8 first subnuvolar, soon became enubilated; and old Sol did
9 not radiate his sudorific caloric so potently as on the
10 hesternal day, but the roads had, in some places, become
11 lutulent and somewhat clarty; presenting a great
12 difficiliation to my incessive velocity, on account of the
13 viscosity of the surface.
14   In consequence of my frequent stoppages, on
15 account of the lutarious and salebrous condition of the trail,
16 I had ample opportunity to exercise my optics upon the
17 aspects of the circumjacent regions. The sinuosities of the
18 vales; the rupellary canons; the titanic, seabrous, nival
19 crested Æonian mountain peaks; the feracity of the terreous
20 surface pertingent to the aqueous meanders, excited in me
21 the greatest oblectation. I arrived one day at a place
22 somewhat multivious; and there being no milliaries, or
23 odometrous stones, I soon became disoriented. In the
24 course of my deambulations, my vision was regaled with an
25 occiduous, floriferous savanna; having in its septentrional,
26 oriental, and austral sections, a slight subsidency. Its
27 terreous surface was a perfect chessom, wholly
28 nonscatebrous. In my transcursion to a designated point,
29 my attention was arrested by the audition of a very puissant
30 sibillation in great proximity to Schnell. He gave a
31 subitaneous resilience. By chary perscrutation, I perceived
32 a fissilingual, batrachophagous, anguine creeple, a crotalus,
33 -circularly recumbent. His cutaneous envelope was
34 squamous, cupreous and fulgid. His caudal extremity was
35 cuspidated with a corneous apex. Schnell made a
36 temerarious supersalient assault upon him, but received

1 darkness   half
2 world   bosom
3 god of dreams
4 stormy   evening
5 accomplished   drying
6 clothes   suitable
7 foot-traveler
8 partly cloudy   cloudless   sun
9 send forth   sweat causing   heat   forcibly
10 yesterday
11 muddy   miry
12 difficulty   forward-progress
13 stickiness
14
15 muddy   rough   road
16 eyes
17 surrounding   windings
18 valleys   cliffy   gorges   immense   rugged   snow
19 capped   everlasting   fertility   earthy
20 adjacent   water   windings
21 delight
22 full of roads   mile boards
23 lost directions
24 wanderings
25 western   flowery   meadow   north
26 east   south   sinking
27 earthy   meadow
28 without springs   passing across
29 hearing   powerful
30 hissing   nearness
31 quick   backward leap   cautious   search
32 forked tongue   frog eating   snake   reptile
33 rattlesnake   lying coiled   skin-covering
34 scaly   coppery   shiny   tail
35 pointed   horny
36 reckless   leaping upon   attack

1 such a siserary upon his rhinal protrusion as immediately
2 induced incessant jactitation. Tumefaction with ineffable
3 celerity became visible in his physical oganization. Being
4 somewhat scient in toxicology and pantagruelism, I
5 administered to him, in the utmost brevity of time,
6 alexiterics, antiphlogistics, and other pharmacy. This
7 treatment produced immediate detumescence and
8 revalescence. Though this assault upon him did not prove
9 exitial, yet, in his resilience from the dipsas he suffered the
10 exarticulation, or rather, the subluxation of his sinistral
11 crural organ; which, in his subsequent circumcursations,
12 extorted the most streperous ejaculations. He soon
13 however, enjoyed complete sanation, and was freed from
14 every traumatic vestige, and relieved of all osteoscope by a
15 nepenthe and antalgics. His subastral vitality has, however,
16 since terminated. Fritz, a castrensian acolythist of mine, an
17 ardent lover of cynegetics and aucupation, made a
18 pteriplegistic venatorial tour, and induced Schnell to
19 accompany him. On the succeeding matin, as they were
20 appropinquating a lapideous and scopulous elevation,
21 Schnell, in his circumcursations, – ventre a terre, – was
22 allected by the fumette of a cache. He there habnab, met a
23 hirsute, hippophagous, sarcophagous, ichthyophagous,
24 melliphagous, insectivorous, vermivorous, frugivorous, and
25 anthropophagous ursine quadruped. A terrific sanguinary
26 cynarctomachy ensued. In the circumgyrations of the
27 battailants, Schnell rendered Bruin excaudate; but Bruin
28 being unguiculated, seized Schnell with one paw by the neb
29 and submaxillary appendage in the hyomental region, and
30 with the other, grasped his capillose dermal integument in
31 the lateral part, and almost exenterated him, and quite
32 suggilated him. By an extra conatus, Schnell effected his
33 eluctation from Bruin; but through hors de combat, his
34 claudication from the arena of concertation, or obluctation,
35 prompted the most puissant ululations. The lancinations,
36 mauger all epulotic, catagmatic and cicatrisive appliances,

28

1   hard blow   nos
2   tossing of the body   swelling   unspeakable
3   quickness   body
4   versed   science of poisons   doctoring
5   shortness
6   poison remedies   remedies for swelling   medicine
7   reduction of swelling
8   recovery
9   fatal   leaping back   snake
10 dislocation   sprain   left-leg
11 running around
12 forced   noisy outeries
13 soundness
14 scar   trace   bone pain
15 pain remedy..remedies to relieve pain..life beneath the stars
16 camp   companion
17 hunting with dogs   bird catching
18 fowl   hunting
19 following   morning
20 nearing   stony   cliffy   bluff
21 running around   scenting on the ground
22 enticed   odor   place for hiding provisions   by chance
23 shaggy   horse   flesh   fish
24 honey   insect   worm   fruit
25 and man eating   bear   bloody
26 dog and bear fight   whirlings
27 contestants   tailless
28 supplied with claws   nose
29 under jaw   front of neck
30 hairy   hide
31 disemboweled
32 beat black and blue   effort
33 escape   out of the fight
34 limping   strife
35 forcible   howling   torn up condition
36 in spite of   skin forming   bone healing   wound curing

1 and all available aciurgical and chirurgical skill, –
2 sphacelated. Interosseal and cervical inturgescence induced
3 angina; terminating in lethality. He was contumulated
4 farantly.
5   After the defuncation, or deperdition of Schnell,
6 being a hippophile, and connusant that equitation is
7 salutiferous, and having by a series of operose
8 bibliopolistic conati, congested an adequacy of pecunious
9 ability to effectuate the emption of, at least, a yawd, I came
10 to the illation to be no longer a peripatetic pedestrian. Just
11 such an equinal servitor as I desiderated, was indigitated to
12 me. He was dandering for pabulation on the verdant gerse
13 of a ranch. Such another caballine quadruped never
14 inspired aerial fluid. He was as obese and glabrous as a
15 fausen; still he had a great inhiation for avenaceous
16 granules. He was perfectly mansuete, and free from
17 calcitration in any attrectation and contrectation of him,
18 with the exception of the taction of clegs. Free from
19 titubation, vessignons, and other defectuosities. His
20 tolutation and his cursorial deliverness, or pernicity on the
21 cespitous champaign are without equipollency or parity. I
22 esayed to bring about an emption of this monture, and
23 persolve therefor, by the offer of a considerable nummulary
24 consideration, and a hypothecation, or oppigneration of my
25 fusee and argental horologue. He was not emptionable.
26 After hospitating for a noctididal period with a vaquero, I
27 entered into a pactitious contract with him. During my
28 tyrociny as vaquero, though not a novice in equitancy, and
29 riding tantivy, yet, in segregating and corraling
30 macrocornous bovines for inustion; in omnium gatherum
31 aggregations, or rodeos; and in abgregating mavericks,–my
32 equestrian acrobatic feats, –vaulting from the dorsal part of
33 bucking bronchos, – was, for a time, truly, mirabile visu.
34 Eventually, in view of the avolation, or evanescence of the
35 aestival and autumnal seasons, and the approximation of

1 Surgical
2 mortified   between the bones   neck swelling
3 quinsy   death   buried
4 decently
5 death   destruction
6 lover of horses   aware   horseback riding
7 health giving   laborious
8 book selling   efforts   accumulated   enough   money
9 accomplish   purchase   ordinary horse
10 conclusion   footman
11 horse   servant   desired   pointed out
12 wandering   food   green   sod
13 farm   horse
14 breathed   air   fat   smooth
15 eel   yearning   oats
16 gentle
17 kicking   handling   touching
18 touch   horseflies
19 stumbling   windgall   defects
20 running   movement   swiftness
21 soddy   plain   equal quality
22 endeavored   purchase   saddle horse
23 pay   money
24 pledging
25 gun   silver   watch   for sale
26 abiding   day and night   cattle man
27 agreement
28 apprenticeship   herdsman   beginner   horsemanship
29 fast riding   separating   penning
30 long horned   cattle   branding   general collections
31 "round ups"   cutting out   strays
32 horseback   high vaulting   bounding   backs
33 Mexican ponies   wonderful to behold
34 flying away   passing away
35 summer   approach

1 brumal gelidity, and cadent niveous particles, -and
2 moreover, being ruricolist rather than an oppidan, I entered
3 in a paction with an occiduous proprietor of a section of
4 terra firma.
5   In conclusion, I will say, – I have today felt
6 somewhat writative, and hence, my present epistolizing is
7 voluminous as Thucydides, and strung out like the caudal
8 appendage of Alcibiades' canine. I have opisthographized
9 much; postillated emendatory criticisms here and there, and
10 added so much paraphrastical marginalia, that, verily –
11 redolet lucernæ.
12   With accustomary comity,
13   Tapeinotatos dulos
14   Ivan

1 winter coldness   falling   snow
2 countryman   townsman
3 contract   western
4 land
5
6 inclined to write
7 Athenian historian   tail
8 dog   twice written upon
9 written corrections on the margins
10 explanatory marginal notes
11 it smells of the lamp
12 usual good will
13 Gr. –most obedient servant

LETTER III
Helianthus Vale, Occident
Dec., 21, 1872

Most Philomathic and Calligraphical Sir:

1   In the finale of my last lucubratory epistolary
2 palimpsest, I gave you cognizance of the verity, that at the
3 inchoation of the pruimous season, I entered into a paction
4 with a certain ponent argricultor. I am not au fait in
5 orthology, but I will essay to impart to you cognition of my
6 position during my commoration with the said excebrous
7 mephistophelian agricolist. Such scleragogy! Such a
8 protraction of vitality! The parvitude of his augeanpulicous
9 habitance! The fuliginous calefactor with cazzon fuel; the
10 rimosity, or fatiscence of its walls; the tenuity of the thoral
11 greith, or integuments, – replete with sanguinivorous
12 cimisses, – are indeed asthenic defensatives against the
13 algidity induced by the frigorific perflations of the Aquilon
14 and the Cæcias.
15   Our edibles, or cagmag, consisted of furfuraceous
16 cakes, azymous jannocks, fusty chitterlings, charqui,
17 lobscouse, and a tenuous insapory puree.
18   The idiopathic microcephalous paterfamilias and
19 dominus of the domicile, is fastuous, brigose, and
20 possessed of a most apodeictical plalanty. He is a genio, – a
21 curioso. A conformity to his punctilious precisianism, is,
22 veritably, a quodlibet. He coerced me to moider during the
23 diurnal period, like a moke, and harassed me with
24 antelucan blaterations. He is multinominous, or
25 polyonomous, as I have multititulated him, Megalophon

sunflower valley   the west

lover of learning   fine penman

1 close   lamplight composed   letter
2 twice written upon   knowledge   fact
3 beginning   frosty   contract
4 western farmer   skilled
5 right description   try   knowledge
6 stay   brainless
7 devilish   farmer   severe discipline
8 smallness   filthy
9 flea abounding home   sooty stove   "buffalo chips"
10 chinkiness   thinness   bed clothes
11 filled   blood devouring bed bugs
12 weak protectives
13 coldness   freezing   blasts   North wind
14 S.E. wind
15 rough diet   bran cakes
16 unleavened bread   musty sausages   jerked beef
17 vegetable hash   thin tasteless soup
18 peculiar   small headed   head of the family
19 master of the shanty   proud   contentious
20 evident self love   peculiar   curious person
21 exact conformance to rule
22 certainly   difficult problem   urged   labor
23 day   donkey
24 before day   senseless noise   much named
25 given many titles to   loud mouthed

1 Fustilugs Dizzard Culion Rodomont Pyrrhonist. His
2 tetricity, carency of bonity-xenodochy³, aphilanthropy,
3 parvanimity, and abnormal anthropophuism, are
4 antipathetical to his vicinal cotemporaries and the metics in
5 his convicinity.
6   As to his proletaneous, abdominous, flavicomous,
7 hypognathous, foveated fraken visaged cepevorous,
8 viragian consort, I have appellated and yclept her, –
9 Oleosity Impudicity Amazon Rixatrix Immundicity. The
10 passing of the macilent Chichevache never agrises or
11 causes her the least horripilation.
12   Having become an acephalist, and fatigated with
13 assiduate superogatory vernile toil, I protracted my
14 obdormition according to autocephalous arbitrament,
15 mauger all his stentorophonic blatterations and
16 perstreperousness to exsuscitate me. This occasioned a
17 rixation which eventuated in my prolating a very
18 dyslogistic sempiternal valediction to his maledicted bye.
19 This was in consension with affectuosity; for I would rather
20 be a mundivagant than a latreutical mercenary, and
21 fraternize with and be ditionary, or subjicible to such an
22 excebrous, abysmally nescient a sept as his.
23   I resumed circumforaneous bibliopolistic functions,
24 and after the profection of about a triduan period
25 subsequent⁴ to prolating my eviturnal adieu to the execrable
26 terraculturist and rancho with a drastic Parthian shot, I
27 approximated and urbiculous community; in the
28 suburbicarian precincts, or purlieus of which I beheld an
29 omniumgatherum rabblement, consisting of queans, giglets,
30 malkins, cinderwenches, galliards, mumpers, skipjacks,
31 beldames, belamours, cuttles, michers, clumps, doodles,
32 nincompoops, cosmopolitans, curmudgeons,
33 ninnyhammers, tatterdemalions, hobbletehoys, and
34 slubberdegullions. All these gave attention to the
35 prestigiations of a thaumaturgical engastrimuth and
36 geomancer. He made the asseveratory declaration that he

1 fatty   blockhead   coward   braggart   disbeliever
2 crabbedness, lack of goodness and hospitality, hatred of others
3 little mindedness   unnatural   human nature
4 repugnant neighbors   sojourners
5 neighborhood
6 having many offspring   yellow haired   long jawed
7 pitted   freckle faced   onion eating
8 noisy   spouse   named
9 greasiness,immodesty,masculine-woman,scold,uncleanlines
10 lean fabulous cow that feeds on patient wives   frightens
11 great trembling horror
12 acknowledger of no superior   very weary
13 continuous   unnecessary   slavish
14 slumbers   independent   decision
15 in spite of   loud mouthed   senseless noise
16 arouse
17 quarrel   ending   bidding
18 uncomplimentary   forever   goodbye   accursed   cabin
19 accord   feelings
20 world wanderer   hired-servant
21 associate   ruled by   subject to
22 brainless   extremely   ignorant   race
23 from house to house   book selling business
24 going forward   three days
25 [subsequent]   after   bidding   forever   accursed
26 clod hopper   hut   forcible   shot on retreat
27 came to   city
28 outskirts   adjacent grounds
29 mixed crowd of the lower classes wenches laughing girls
30 drabs   drudges   gay men   beggars   upstarts
31 old women gallants idlers stupid fellows triflers
32 sillyfellows   ramblers   misers
33 half wits   ragtags   gawky boys
34 slovens
35 foretelling   wonder telling   ventriloquist
36 fortune teller   positive

37

1 could give ocular apodixis that he possessed complete
2 cognition of metoposcopy, ophthalmoscopy, chiromancy,
3 rhabdomancy, astragalomancy, arithmancy, capnomancy,
4 and onomancy. He averred that he was an adept
5 oneirocritic, cultrivorist, and funambulist.
6   The ariolation and recluding the future terrestrial
7 allotments of the congeries that environed this pseudo-
8 omniscious mirabilary, effectuated singular phases in their
9 phizes. Those who, by a spectation either into aqueous
10 liquids, or upon the nodosities of a caduceus or upon the
11 corrugations of their mannal extremities, or by any other
12 media of auguration, or vaticination, were favored with a
13 perception of their future beatitude, became salient with
14 delectation, and emitted the most obstreperous
15 cachinnations; whilst others, beholding either their
16 proximity to the irremeable bourne, or much amaritude
17 immixed with the evolutions of the filaments of their
18 sublunary vitality, became quite cogitabund, atrabilarian,
19 queremonious, pessimistic, and exacerbated.
20   Leaving the fatiloquent flabbergaster and his dupes,
21 and desiderating the deletion of nescience, as also the
22 impletion of my nummulary crumenal with rhino, whilst
23 hiemating, – for, as you know, *absque argento omnia vano,*
24 – I decided to demonstrate my didacticity by becoming a
25 propædeutical domine; and hence, I entered into a
26 synallagmatic astipulation as rural pedagogue. So soon as
27 the requisite subsignations could be secured to the bipartite
28 stipendiary syngraph, I entered the phrontistery, and
29 assumed paideutical and chrestomathic functions.
30   About the time of my becoming an erudiating
31 literator of frontier bairns, I resorted to an umbratical
32 castrametation containing multitudinous audients;
33 addressed by a homilist. The sere autumnal season; the
34 dense tenebrious umbrosity of the bushet; and the
35 moliminous occasion of the comportation, were conducent
36 to the exsuscitation of pietism, or epicedian emotions. The

1 sight-proof   knowledge
2 foretelling from the face   eyes   hands
3 rods   dice   figures   smoke
4 and names   asserted   expert
5 dream interpreter   knife swallower   rope walker
6 foretelling   unfolding
7 crowd   surrounded   false
8 all knowing   wonder teller   caused   appearances
9 faces   looking   water
10 knots   rod
11 wrinkles   hands
12 means   foretelling   prophecy
13 happiness   leaping
14 delight   sent forth   noisy
15 hysterical laughter
16 nearness   undiscovered country   bitterness
17 unrolling   threads
18 beneath the moon life   deeply thoughtful   melancholy
19 complaining   gloomy   irritated
20 wonder telling   predictor
21 wishing   blotting out   ignorance
22 filling   money purse   money
23 passing the winter   [Lat.] Without money all is vain.
24 aptness to teach
25 primary   school master
26 reciprocal contract   country-teacher
27 necessary-signatures   double
28 for salary   contract signed by all interested   schoolhouse
29 duties of teaching useful subjects
30 instructing
31 educator   children   shady-encampment
32 many   listeners
33 preacher   dry
34 gloomy   shade
35 important   assembly   helpful   awakening
36 devotion   mournful

1 abearance, ostent, and physiognomical aspects of the
2 ecclesiasts present, furnished a roboration of the already
3 generated saturnity.
4   The anteriority of the officiating homilist's
5 existence had been rather sinuous and protean. His
6 juvenility had been maculated with many vicious,
7 triobolary extravagations and nefandous abominations. At
8 the termination of his adolescence, he became a fustilarian,
9 a scambler, a literator, an arpentator, an acutiator, a
10 horologist, and an omnivagant under the profession of
11 chiropodist, bletonist, and vulcanian journeyman. By an
12 esoteric and imaginary supernal influence, he was speedily
13 transformed into an entheastic pietist; and he transferred the
14 acumen of his mental vision from secular and terrene
15 objects, into cryptic and acroamatical parts of the
16 hagiography. Surcharged with bibliomania, he was
17 propense to bibliomancy. He was a thorough solifidian
18 catabaptist and saturnist; – and I may adject, a mere
19 theologaster, – an empirical idiopathic suist. His hierology
20 was on the appropinquation of the chiliastic empyrosis of
21 this mundane oblate spheroid, or macrocosm, based on the
22 fatidical parts of the hierography.
23   His farrand of allocution was sui generis.
24   Notwithstanding his boasted opsimathy, the
25 illiteracy and inurbanity of the precedaneous part of his life
26 were very tralucent. His intonations were dolorous, and in
27 the mobility of his corporeity he resembled a funambulist.
28 In his elocution, his vocal powers ascended from an almost
29 inaudible susurration to crocitation, and from crocitation to
30 such a cacophonic vociferation as made him dreul, and was
31 puissant enough to laniate his guttural orifice. His cadences
32 terminated in mere raucous susurrations. His defectuous
33 mimesis of Whitefield was quite perceptible. In his
34 eclaircissement of the vaticinal portion of the hagiography
35 in relation, eschatologically, – to the chiliastic finale of this
36 mundane structure, he made certain occurrences

1 deportment   appearance   countenances
2 preachers   strengthening
3 solemnity
4 former part   preacher
5 crooked   changeful
6 youth   stained   mean
7 worthless   excesses   very great wickedness
8 youth   scoundrel
9 sponge   school master   surveyor   razor grinder
10 clock mender   tramp
11 corn doctor   water wizard   traveling smith
12 mysterious   from above
13 inspired   religionist
14 keenness   mind sight   temporal   earthly
15 hidden   profound
16 sacred writings   filled   book mania
17 inclined   book divining   faith believing
18 antibaptist   very grave person   add
19 divinity quack, experimenting, peculiar, self loving bigot, discourse
20 approach   millennial   conflagration
21 earth   great world
22 prophetic   sacred writings
23 manner   address   self peculiar
24 education late in life
25 ignorance   unpolished manners   former
26 evident   voice modulation   doleful
27 movements   body   rope walker
28 oratory   voice
29 unheard   whispers   croaking
30 harsh   loud shouting   froth at the mouth
31 forcible   rend   throat   lowering of voice
32 harsh   whispers   imperfect
33 imitation   Eng. Meth. Revivalist
34 explanation   prophetic   sacred writings
35 as to final causes   millennial termination
36 earth

1 chronologically synchronous, or equitemporaneous, which
2 glossologists and authentic historiographers greatly
3 eloigned from each other. In his epilogisms in relation to
4 fatidical events, he evinced an aspernation of all
5 embolisms.
6   He gave an anagogical, chimerical, and acataleptic
7 interpretation to prophetical icons, which all noetic
8 elucidators have perpended as literal. In verity, his
9 cacodoxical hierology was so replete with anfractuosities,
10 pseudological fallencies, prochronisms, isochronisms,
11 parachronisms, and illogicalities, that the entirety of the
12 matter became dubitable, ancipitable, and quite
13 amphigorical to me, notwithstanding the fact his sapient
14 connictations in the formation of his ergotisms, seemed to
15 exhibit his plerophory of assurance that the proximity of
16 the empyrosis was no longer a dubiosity, or synchretistical
17 quodlibet. His parenetical epilogation seized the cullibility
18 of his atechnic audients, and greatly exagitated them.
19   The plateau of castrametation was quiquepartite.
20 The one anent, or paravant the ambo, or rostrum, having a
21 sepiment for demarkation^5, had a stramineous, or festucous
22 surface for the occupancy of the sequents and questants. In
23 juxtaposition to this, were dualistic departments for the
24 gent, farant, and debonair auditors. Posterior to these, were
25 to for the bisexous rabblement, or plebeiance. The male
26 department of the latter was fraught with – faitours,
27 fopdoodles, boolies, louts, claw backs, kickshoes,
28 petitmaitres, ragabashes, rakehells, rampallians, bumpkins,
29 jackanapes, wassailers, and nincompoops.
30   The feminine department was stocked with jilts,
31 flirtigigs, fizzigs, malkins, mauthers, modders, tomrips,
32 demireps, flibbergibs, and gamerstangs.
33   The occupants of these two departments mutually
34 nictated at their lemen, and exhibited the most derisory
35 deport towards the homilist. Indeed, the jouissance,
36 enterparlance, and effrenation of this posse were a great

1 happen at the same time
2 interpreters   reliable-historians
3 separated   computations
4 prophetical   showed   contempt
5 inserted time
6 mystical   imaginary   incomprehensible
7 representations   intelligent-interpreters
8 considered   fact
9 doctrinally wrong, discourse, filled, windings and turnings
10 mistakes   giving dates too early   in equal time
11 too late   wrong reasoning
12 doubtful   double meaning
13 nonsensical   wise
14 winking   reasonings
15 full confidence   nearness
16 great conflagration   matter of doubt
17 irreconcilable-problem, summing up, exhortation, credulity
18 uneducated   hearers   aroused
19 high level ground   encampment   fivefold
20 next to   in front of   pulpit
21 partition   separation   strawy   chaffy
22 follower   seekers
23 adjoining   double
24 decent   handsome   respectable   hearers
25 of both sexes   common people
26 scoundrels
27 insignificant fellows,tramps,mean fellows,flatterers,dancers
28 fops   rag tags   dissolutes   impertinents   half wits
29 upstarts   revelers   fools
30 coquettes
31 flirts, gadders, servants, foppish girls, fast girls, flatterers
32 giddy girls
33
34 winked   sweethearts   scornful-behavior
35 preacher   merriment
36 talking   rowdyism   crowd

1 crux to the proximate audients. At this apathistical posse,
2 the periscopic, argus eyed preachman made prepotent
3 conatus.
4 Although in this isagogical part of his discourse, he
5 disclaimed even a velleity towards decertation with any of
6 his cotemporaries, yet he delitigated Hulotheism,
7 Islamism, and Papism, and increpated iconolators.
8 His fervency became apparent in his aparithmesis,
9 and as he approximated the epilogue, or parenetical part,
10 and epiphonema of his homily.
11 His parenesis was calid. I will append to the
12 antecedent portraiture an excerpt from my itinerary as
13 noted down by me brachygraphically.
14 My dear sectators: – implore you to cherish
15 eupathy, and a plenary fructure of religion. Morigerate no
16 longer your ingenerate malign propensions. Enter upon
17 theopathy, and abnegate your mundanity and secularity.
18 You can yet have a pregustation, yea, a prelibation of a
19 better existence.
20 O, ye apathistical laodiceans! Soon, – it may be
21 hodiurnal, – your psychomachy will terminate, and your
22 foy be transmuted into fruition. Evitate all alamodality and
23 recidivation; and to this end, indagate the hagiography with
24 perseverant incessancy in relation to the verity of these
25 announcements. Secern yourselves from all ludibrious
26 rabblements, and seek supersecular indefectible treasures.
27 Have your cressets and flambeaus luminously flagrant, and
28 evitate invigilance. But O, ye fatours, sycophantic
29 parasites, and flibbergibs; ye sterquilinous rakehells,
30 rampallians, wassailers, flirtigigs, and demireps! What
31 hortation shall I impart to you? You all lie under divine
32 execration, and your subastral existence is truly
33 probationary and temporaneous. Divest yourselves of your
34 imbonity, adiaphorism, incogitancy, and malversation.
35 Bonity is impetrable. Perpend your longinquity from

1 vexation   nearest   hearers   indifferent
2 all around seeing   sharp eyed   strong
3 effort
4 introductory
5 least desire   controversy   persons living
6 at same time, spoke against, doctrine that matter is God
7 Mohammedism   rebuked   image worshippers
8 final summing up
9 neared   concluding remarks
10 exhortation   sermon
11 exhortation   fervent
12 foregoing   description   extract   record of travels
13 in shorthand
14 brethren   entreat
15 right feeling   full enjoyment   obey
16 inborn   wicked   inclinations
17 religious suffering   deny   worldliness   temporal things
18 foretaste
19
20 indifferent   lukewarm in religion
21 today   contest of flesh and spirit
22 faith, changed, realization, avoid, conformity to the world
23 backsliding   search the scriptures
24 persevering constancy   truth
25 separate   low vulgar society
26 heavenly   unfading
27 lamps   and torches brightly ablaze
28 lack of watchfulness   evil doers   flattering
29 sponges   sycophants   filthy   debauchees
30 mean wretches   drunkards   flirts   fast girls
31 advice
32 curse   below stars
33 on trial, for a time, quit your meanness, rid yourselves of
34 religious indifference   thoughtlessness   bad conduct
35 goodness in obtaining by prayer, consider, great distance

1 eupathy, and the inenarrable sequences of your
2 impreparation from the appropinquating catastrophe.
3   O, ye supercilious petitmaitres! Conculcate the
4 fulgid ornature of your persons, and suppress your
5 nugacities, and stultiloquy. Ye kickshoes! Cease your
6 tripudiations. Ye wassailers! Elide your costrels, and
7 denegate yourselves of your vinolency, and cretan
8 practices. Ye modders, and fopdoodles; and ye clinquant
9 flirts! Abject your elamping, bombycinous habiliments, and
10 your bijoutry, and cease your irrational calamistrations.
11 And O, ye covetous and covinous hunks! ye terrigenous
12 sept! Desist from your supervacaneous toil and
13 disquietudes.
14   Accede ye all into the stramineous department
15 paravant the rostrum. Incurvate your poplitics, and perform
16 genuflection. Obsecrate that you may impetrate a purgation
17 from all your nefandous piacles and abominations, and
18 become impeccable. If you refuse to come, you will be in a
19 periclitation to suffer irremeable relegation to the
20 cimmerian inframundane Stygian and Acherontic regions
21 of Abaddon, where your apprecations and your quiritations
22 will be frustraneous, and horrendous sulphureous
23 flagrations will circumgyrate about you, and interminable
24 remordency will excruciate you sempiternally.
25   At this juncture, the influx into the paleous
26 department became ample and rapid. Conclamations,
27 lachrymations, and perstreperous boations became
28 apparently, ubiquitous and omnipresential. The synchysis,
29 durdum, and quassation of the synaxis were, according to
30 my standard of religious credenda, very absonant, and
31 malapropos, and ergo, I made my exit.
32   Subsequently, I enjoyed commensation with this
33 concionator at a sybaritic fete, where he evinced himself an
34 expert ornithotomist, and a sapient deipnosophist and
35 cyclopedic sitiologist, but indicated his undivested
36 thraldom to gastronomy.

1 right feeling   indescribable   results
2 unreadiness   approaching sudden calamity
3 proud fops   trample under foot
4 glittering ornaments
5 bad behavior   foolishness   dancers
6 dancing   revelers   dash to pieces   bottles
7 deny   wine drinking   lying
8 gaily dressed fops, dressed in tinsel finery, flirts cast off
9 glittering silken attire
10 trinkets   unnatural hair curling
11 niggardly   dishonest   misers   earthborn set
12 needless
13
14 come   strawy
15 opposite   pulpit   bend   knee joints
16 kneeling in prayer, entreat, obtain by prayer, cleansing
17 heinous crimes   wickedness
18 free from sin
19 great danger   unreturnable banishment
20 fearfully dark underworld infernal   gloomy
21 bottomless pit   cries for help   wailings
22 unavailing   horrid   brimstone
23 flames   roll and whirl   unending
24 remorse   torment   forever and ever
25 inflow   chaffy
26 shouts of many
27 weeping   noisy   uproar
28 everywhere   at all places
29 confusion   noise   shaking
30 congregation   articles of faith   contrary
31 out of place   therefore   departure
32 eating at same table
33 luxurious   dining   proved
34 bird dissector   wise   table conversationalist
35 extensively learned in science of diet   unrestrained
36 bondage   gluttony

1   Deeming this a suffisance of my arcane bombastry
2 for the present,
3   I am,
4   Most amicably and subserviently,
5   Ivan

1   enough   difficult to understand "big words"

LETTER IV
Spermophile Champaign, Occident
Jan. 15, 1873

Most Autodidactic and Pedagogical Sir: –

1   As my vocabulary of lexiphanic and sesquipedal
2 polysyllabicities is not yet exhausted, I again merge my
3 plumous implement of chirography into the atramental
4 fluid for another effusion of epistolary fustian.
5   A few fortnights prior to the advent of the hiemal
6 season, I, in consociation with Fritz, – a contubernial
7 belamy of mine, – returning from an intermontane venatory
8 excursion, espied in the convicinity of an oppidan
9 community, an ample concourse of the populacy in an
10 apert, procere, and foliaceous frith, giving audition to a
11 political nestorian sermocinator.
12   He was a septuagenary; and being a contuberant, he
13 was a questant for their suffrages at their proximous, or
14 prochein ballotation, for nomothetical dignity.
15   He was rugose, pachydermatous, slightly bisson,
16 breviped, tardigradous, and affected with partial surdity,
17 secutiency, caducity, and perceptible seity.
18 Archaisms, exoticisms, exolete and obsolescent lingo, and
19 fetichistic chauvinism, characterized his allocution to the
20 conflux.
21   He located the prelation of himself to his
22 competitors, upon the chevisances of the antecedaneous
23 part of his existence; upon his connusance of cameralistics,
24 chrematistics, and jurisprudence; upon his consension with

50

self taught   school teaching

1 word list   pedantic
2 long many syllabled words   dip
3 writing pen   ink
4 outpour   letter   bombast
5 weeks   before   coming   winter
6 company   tent companion
7 among the mountains   hunting trip
8 neighborhood   town
9 assembly
10 open   tall-leafy-grove   attention
11 wise from age   speaker
12 70 years old   candidate
13 seeker   votes   next
14 election   legislative honors
15 wrinkled   thick skinned   near sighted
16 short legged   slow   paced   deafness
17 dimness of sight   feebleness of age   peculiarity
18 words out of date, foreign, out of use, expressions out use
19 excessively devoted   extravagant patriotism   address
20 assembly
21 preference
22 achievements   former
23 knowledge   sciences of finance
24 wealth and juridical law   agreement

1 the primordial and immaculate democracy; and especially
2 upon his senility and proleptical resipiscence.
3   In the enumeration of his chevisances, he furnished
4 an ocular apodixis, that he was of a douty and ethel stirp.
5 His ayle and eame had both been bellipotent, and of his
6 progenitors had been consessor with the thesmothetes of
7 our nation during the formation of the national systasis, and
8 rendered much adminicular service. He was himself a ci-
9 devant achillean cid, or chiliarch of a vexillation, and for
10 many annuary epochs, endured the durity of agminal
11 castrametation, and wielded the bilbo in multitudinous
12 armisonous valkyrian concertations, upon sanguifluous
13 arenas.
14   These things were not thrasonically spoken. He
15 averred that his connusance of cameralistics had been utile
16 to the federal compact on various emergencies. He made
17 the indiction that an ampliation of the tariff upon forinsecal
18 commodities would induce remote gubernations to
19 recalcitrate by passing interdictory laws in relation to us;
20 and as a sequence, a decurtation of our mercatantes would
21 occur.
22   His advocacy of a minoration of the tariff upon
23 forinsecal mercature was pancratic. His consension with the
24 primevous democraty, and his resipiscence from
25 adolescence to a great provexity, were very luculent.
26   His principia are: – The minoration of all
27 extravagations and sumptuosities in hegemonical
28 operations, especially the supervacaneous guerdons of the
29 gubernative functionaries; the eversion of pecunious
30 synomosies; the abrogation of all the dysnomies of the
31 present dynasts; the cessation of the mercature on
32 mutatious media; the enactment of isonomies; the
33 depulsion of vitiosity in the proletarian ranks by the
34 enactment of salutiferous laws; the deletion of popular
35 inscience, by the erection of phrontisteries of all gradations.
36 In the inferior, or propædeutical, superior and ulterior of

1 original   untainted
2 great age   far seeing-experience
3 achievements
4 sight proof   illustrious-noble-family
5 grandfather   uncle   mighty in war
6 ancestors   associate   lawgivers
7 constitution
8 assistant
9 at one time, very brave, commander, company of soldiers
10 years   hardships   army
11 encampment   sword   many
12 resounding with arms   hard fought battles   blood-
13 flowing battlefields
14 boastfully
15 asserted   knowledge   finance   profitable
16 times of need
17 declaration   charges on foreign imported goods   foreign
18 nations
19 kickback   prohibitory
20 result   cutting off   foreign merchants
21
22 decrease   duty
23 foreign merchandise   very forcible   agreement
24 early   democracy   hard earned experience
25 youth   great age   very clear
26 main principles   decrease
27 extravagances   high living   controlling
28 needless   salaries
29 government officials   overthrow   monied
30 political clubs   repeal   bad laws
31 "bosses"   trade
32 borrowed capital   equal laws
33 driving away   wickedness   lower ranks
34 wholesome laws   blotting out
35 ignorance   schoolhouses
36 primary   intermediate and advanced

1 which should be taught,-orthography, chirogaphy,
2 orthoepy, aretology, ontology, physianthropy,
3 pathognomy, aristology, ophthalmology, deontology,
4 geogony, geography, geology, geognosy,
5 geoscopy, oryctognosy, zoography, trochilics, taxidermy,
6 pneumatology, agrostology, economics, longimetry,
7 hydrodynamics, agriology, gymnastics, psychology,
8 dietetics, electrobiology, and anthroposophy.
9   He iterated the asseveration, that he was not a
10 questant for a participation in the gubernance of the
11 federation in view of ditation; but rather, from an
12 irrepressible conviction that a mutation in the regnant
13 powers should take place; that the extravagations and
14 largitations of the incumbent dynasts have effectuated a
15 labefaction of former eutaxy; that his former longanimity
16 was exhausted; that, although longevous, he had never, in
17 any anteriority of his subcelestial being, perceived such a
18 necessitation for a decurtation of national fallencies as in
19 this present secle. He made the indication, that the present
20 dysnomy and aspect of the federation was most luctual to
21 him; and that, as a statist, he had the most sombre
22 ominations of disastrous sequences in view of the
23 maladministration, depeculations, and proditions of the
24 gubernative party; that he had an insatiable inhiation to
25 witness the reddition and prepotency of pure
26 Washingtonian and Jeffersonian democracy, or ochlocracy;
27 and never, plutocracy[6].
28   In the prevenient, or prolegomenary part of his
29 locution, the orator at times haffled somewhat, but he soon
30 became grandiloquent. His senectitude, and the vestiges of
31 anterior debonairity, furnished an essoin for his frequent
32 eructations and exspuitions.
33   His epilogue was apothegmatical, and abounded in
34 magniloquence, facundity, aristarchian and escharotic
35 pasquinade.

1 spelling   writing
2 pronunciation,treatises on virtue,causes of being,human life
3 the passions, dining, eye diseases, duty
4 formation of the earth, description of the earth, earth's structure, earth's composition
5 soil   minerals   animals   wheel work   stuffing skins
6 elastic fluids   grasses   household affairs   distances
7 water power   savages   bodily exercise   mind
8 diet   animal electricity   character from face
9 repeated   declaration
10 seeker   administration
11 union   getting rich
12 change-ruling
13 extravagances
14 giving presents   rulers in office   caused
15 weakening   good laws   patience
16 very old
17 former part   life below stars
18 curtailing   follies
19 century   declaration
20 bad laws   sad
21 statesman   gloomy
22 forebodings
23 bad management   robberies   treachery
24 controlling   very craving   desire
25 return   ruling power
26 government by common people
27 rich
28 first   introductory
29 address   faltered
30 eloquent   great age   traces
31 former   civility   excuse
32 belching   spitting
33 closing remarks   pithy
34 lofty speaking   eloquence   severely critical   caustic
35 lampoon

1   I will subjoin a paraphrastical version of it as
2 tachygraphically jotted down in my adversaria.
3   O, my compatriots and my constituency! Do you
4 not espy a crisis in your subastral vitality, in which you
5 should depel your lethal incogitancy, and precogitate your
6 ballotation? Remember you are plenipotent, aye,
7 multipotent to strangulate the malign assuetudes and
8 abutions of the incumbent dynasts. Armipotent to prevent a
9 new bevy of parasitical politicasters to convive upon you
10 like so many sanguisuges upon insensate quadrupeds. My
11 competitors are nothing but empiric neonomians, sciolistic
12 parvenues, neoterics, inflated neophytes to their party,
13 jackadandies; ostentous, and unwilling to moile. They are
14 far more cognizant and scient in cicisbeanism than in civil
15 economics and jurisprudence. Their collimation is to be the
16 beau monde, and saginate their macilent microcosms on the
17 cess of the leod. They are mere covinous slangwhangers
18 and skipkennels to a radical junto; mere machivellian
19 wealsmen, whose sermocinations are nothing but
20 teratological blandiloquence and illecebrous demagogism.
21   They are as inane of true civism as the Russian
22 autocrat is of canailleism. I obtestate you, my senile and
23 junior democratists, to redintegrate the dimication for the
24 eversion of radicalism, and for the rehabilitation of
25 primordiate omniparity in the republic. Recall to your
26 souvenance the pollicitations of the present regents and
27 their entire inanity. Would you not rather be under a
28 gerontocracy, a neocracy, a stratocracy, a pantisocracy, or
29 even a gynecocracy, than under glavering radicalism and
30 republican timocracy? I conjure you to be thoroughstitches
31 in your colluctancy to radical dition. I obsecrate you to
32 abject your antecedaneous segnitude; to indenizen the
33 aliens, and be movent.
34   Let the vexillaries antecede the gradient column
35 with flotant vexils inscribed with – "EUNOMY AND
36 OMNIPARITY!"

1 Simplified
2 in short hand   notebook
3 fellow citizens   supporters
4 behold   decisive moment   life below stars
5 cast aside   fatal   thoughtlessness   premeditate
6 voting   fully able
7 altogether able   evil-customs
8 abuses   in office "bosses"   powerful in arms
9 swarm   fawning   petty politicians   feast
10 bloodsuckers   dumb beasts
11 experimenting   wishers for change   little knowing
12 upstarts   novices   puffed up   new converts
13 fops   proud   labor
14 knowing   versed in   dangling about women
15 managing public affairs   juridical law   chief aim
16 fashionable world   fatten   lean   little world
17 tax   people   dishonest   vulgar mouths
18 pleasers of the vulgar   faction   politically cunning
19 politicians   speeches
20 high sounding, flattery, enticing, leading of common people
21 ignorant   citizenship
22 absolute   ruler   common people   entreat   aged
23 younger democrats   renew   contest
24 overthrow   restoration
25 original   general equality
26 remembrance   promises   rulers
27 emptiness
28 government by old men   new officials   military   by all
29 by women   flattering
30 rich rulers   earnestly implore   hustlers
31 resistance   subjection   be
32 throw aside   heretofore   indifference   naturalize the
33 foreigners   on the move
34 standard bearers   go before   walking
35 flying banners   GOOD LAWS AND
36 EQUAL RIGHTS

1   Let all the suffragists advene to the arena of

2 ballotation for the ereption of the munities of the plurality

3 from the abutions and proditions of the incumbent

4 plutocrats.

5   Let the radicals quassate like Belshazzar, and

6 realize ubiquitary exauctoration, extraversion, ostracism

7 and atimy!

8   This peroration made the whole contesseration

9 animose, and elicited an euge potent enough to lacerate

10 one's auricular avenues.

11   The political comportation then disbanded.

12   At this point, Fritz, – my chum, – encountered the

13 compellation of an apparitor with a capias, or interpellation

14 for him to appear at the proxime judicatory to give

15 reponsion to certain allegata divulgated by a certain

16 ranchero, delator.

17   He delated Fritz of clancular depulsion, ablastion,

18 deportation and vendition of rotherbeasts. This seemed to

19 impinge Fritz like fulmination and fulguration; and at first,

20 greatly tristitiated him. In a peregrine land, without many

21 belamies, he was in a great prosternation relative to his

22 situation. He however, found a mainpernor. The day of

23 pervestigation, – juridicus dies – soon arrived. Fritz, being

24 an alien, unkent, with limited pecuniary resources, a

25 legulian became the ultroneous susceptor of his cause.

26   This somatic physique was procere and beatous, and

27 his ostent, debonair. Multiscious in vitilitigation and

28 alethiology; omnipercipient, pansophical, emissitous, and

29 obversant with anthroposcopy, metoposcopy, and

30 dialetics. Without dubitancy, he was a dabster, a

31 philalethist, a cyclopedic quodlibetarian, and an areopagist.

32   His responsion to the isagogical speech of the

33 microcephalous jurist for the regime, was consentaneous

34 with true placitory dialectics, and was such a pancratic

35 cassation of the paralogy of his antiloquist, that all

36 pendency relative to Fritz's being a larcener was douted.

1 voters   advance
2 voting grounds   snatching away   natural rights   majority
3 abuses   treachery
4 rich rulers in office
5 tremble with fear
6 general turning out of office, rejection, political banishment
7 public disgrace
8 exhortation   assembly
9 excited   brought forth   applause   powerful   rend
10 ear drums
11 assembly
12
13 address   officer   writ of arrest   summons
14 next   court of justice
15 answer   criminal charges   made known
16 ranchman   accuser
17 charged   secretly   taking and driving away
18 shipping   selling   black cattle
19 strike   thunder and lightening
20 dejected   strange
21 good friends   depression
22 bondsman
23 trial   court day
24 stranger   unknown   bank account
25 lawyer   voluntary   defender
26 bodily structure   tall   handsome
27 manner   pleasing   well versed   law contests
28 science of truth, very observant, thoroughly educated, very watchful
29 familiar with human nature   knowing character from face
30 logical reasoning   doubt   expert
31 lover of truth, conversant on all subjects, member of supreme court
32 reply   introductory
33 little headed   lawyer   plaintiff   in accord
34 judicial pleadings   powerful
35 making void   false reasonings   opponent suspense
36 thief   extinguished

1   The jurist for the polity was a mere charlatanical
2 champertor. His cadaverous, rugose, cataphysical, and
3 verrucose phiz; his camoused olfactor; his extuberant
4 labials; his dolichocephalous, cirrigerous,-somewhat
5 ulotrichous, informous noll; his myopy and strabism; his
6 edentated, nicotian moe; his macrognathic, barbigerous
7 mazard; his macilent corporeity; the exility and marcidity
8 of his macropodous locomotives; all premonstrated his
9 herbetude, and was axiomatic evidence that he was not
10 even a mediocrist, but a mere inerudite, atechnic,
11 polygrammatical hafter and pervicacious barrator. His
12 inscience of avitous justicements, and alethiology, and his
13 perissology and his battology imparted to his tractation of
14 his cause an imperspicuity which rendered it immomentous
15 to his juratory audients.
16   The catastasis, or preludious part of his apertion of
17 the accrimination was ambagitory, and catachrestical. His
18 incapacity was apodeictically conspicuous in the adduction,
19 adjuration, and scissitation of this pseudo testificators.
20   They were a mendacious clan, and their
21 testifications were very absonous, and devoid of all
22 comprobation. In verity, the mendacity of some of the
23 testificators was so diaphanous that Fritz's propugnor
24 obtained from the domesman, or eirenarch, the right of
25 compurgation, by the adduction of adscititious evidence
26 relative to some of them as deponents. In this adduction of
27 adminicular testimony, no compurgators appeared. In the
28 final mediety of his locution, there was no concatenation of
29 roborant circumstances, but a mere consarcination of
30 commentitious allegata, which could never constitute a
31 miniment of any nefandous piacle or anomy in Fritz.
32   After many supervacaneous iterations of mere
33 fingle fangle, he commenced to supparasite the juratory
34 bevy relative to their noetical habilitation to sarse Fritz's
35 maleficence, and adjudicate to ablegate him to a lobspound,
36 and have him there immured and securely obserated; or

1 prosecution   nondescript
2 buyer of lawsuits   pale   wrinkled   deformed
3 warty   face   flat   nose
4 projecting lips   negro headed   curly
5 frizzy   ill shaped head   hear sightedness   squinting
6 toothless   ambiered   mouth   long jawed   bearded
7 chin   lean   body   thinness   leanness
8 long legs   foreshowed
9 stupidity   very plain
10 medium ability   unlearned   ignorant
11 officious wrangler   contrary strife maker
12 ignorance   ancient court proceedings   evidence of truth
13 needless repetitions   superfluous words   handling
14 want of clearness   of no importance
15 jury
16 introductory   preliminary   opening
17 accusation   indirect   far fetched
18 plainly to be seen   bringing forward
19 administering oaths   questioning   false witnesses
20 lying   clique
21 evidence   contradictory   lacking
22 agreement   fact   lying
23 witnesses   clear   defender
24 judge
25 verification of oaths   bringing forward   supplemental
26 witnesses   introduction
27 aiding   persons swearing to veracity of others
28 latter half   speech   connection
29 strengthening   patchwork
30 imaginary   accusations
31 least trifle   heinous crime   law violation
32 needless   repetitions
33 nonsense   flatter   jury
34 intellectual   qualifications   sift out
35 meanness   decide judicially   send   prison
36 shut up   locked in

1 mulct him to such a pecuniary amount as to make the
2 adeption of the fidejussor impracticable; thereby effecting
3 his relegation from the convicinity.
4   Thus he dawdled; and such was his insulsity,
5 morology, jejunity, and the nebulosity of his harns, that he
6 could not perceive the derisive ludification of his audients.
7   He seemed to be inimicitous and acerb toward Fritz
8 in his agrestic russet, through mere prosopolepsy.
9   The replication of Fritz's legist to this badinage,
10 notwithstanding his pauciloquy, was anatreptic, elenctrical,
11 prepotent, and replete with the most pyrotic pasquinade. He
12 eclaircised all the nodose aspects in the accrimination, and
13 evinced Fritz's columbine innocency; that the delator's
14 testificators were a most mendacious cretan sept; that the
15 delation contained a plenitude of pseudologies and
16 maledicencies; and that the querent was an egotistical
17 morosoph, and dedolent scelerat; prompted wholly in the
18 delation by an indomitable misanthropy and philistinism;
19 and that he was entitled to a nihility, or nullibeity. In verity,
20 that the entire procedure was illegal; and that, from
21 precognita, and precedence he demanded not only an
22 absolutory acquittal, an unextorted assoilzie and
23 deraignment. Not only so, but a considerable pecuniary
24 assythment, as Fritz's absolute, and jural droit.
25   The arbitrament, or adjudication of the judicature
26 was proficuous to Fritz. In a jiffy, the whole comportation
27 emitted into the aerial vault the most conclamatory and
28 congratulatory boations, and effunded upon the ranchero
29 the plethoric cornu-copia[7] of their ire. The redacteurs and
30 diurualists gave Fritz's arraignment and the adjudication,
31 divulgation and evulgation; which invested him with
32 molimiuous and imperdible famosity.
33   More anon.
34   Most immutably,
35   Amicus tuus,
36   Ivan

1 fine   money
2 obtaining   bondsman
3 banishment   neighborhood
4 wasted time   stupidity
5 nonsense   barrenness   cloudiness   brains
6 mocking fun making   hearers
7 unfriendly   embittered
8 country dress   judging character from dress
9 reply   attorney   senseless talk
10 [multum in parvo]   few words   overpowering   refuting
11 very forcible   filled   burning   sarcasm
12 made clear   knotty   accusation
13 clearly showed   dovelike   accuser's
14 witnesses   untruthful   lying   set
15 accusations   abundance   falsehoods
16 slanders   plaintiff   selfish
17 learned fool   remorseless   scoundrel
18 accusation   incontrollable   hatred of mankind and culture
19 nonexistence   fact
20
21 things known   authoritative examples
22 free from blame discharge   unforced   setting free
23 judicially   money
24 damages   just and natural right
25 decision   verdict   court
26 favorable   all at once   assembly
27 sent forth   laud hurrahs
28 well wishing noisy demonstrations   poured out   ranchman
29 very full   horn of plenty   anger   reporters
30 editors   trial
31 publicity   published abroad   clothed
32 very important   indestructible   notoriety
33
34 unchangeably
35 [Lat.] your friend

LETTER V
Artemisia Arroyo, Occident
Feb. 19, 1873

Most scribatious and altruistic Sir:-

1   Being again moved with something like cacœthes
2 scribendi, I call into requisition my escritorial furnishments
3 to delineate for you, in minutiæ, my experience at a
4 sybaritic nuptial ambigu, and the concomitant momentous
5 sequences.
6   Fritz and I returning from a negotiatory trip to the
7 hesperian megalopolis, arrived, in the post-meridian part of
8 the day, in a visne.
9   Having approximated a hostelry of imposing and
10 delectable appearance, we discovered that every
11 concomitant of the establishment was undergoing a general
12 depuration. All the factotums about the hacienda were
13 sedulously employed. I made a circumspective pedetentous
14 reconnoitering tour of inspection to the posterior
15 department of the extruction, where I espied the most
16 sanguinary scenes. There took place the trucidation of
17 pennigerous bipeds by decollation; of vituline, ovine,
18 curvicaudate suilline, or porcine, and other crinigerous and
19 lanigerous quadrupeds, by the exantlation of their
20 sanguineous fluid. Some of the plumigerous and aligerous
21 bipeds were undergoing deplumation, or deprivation of
22 their induments by decerption.
23   Some of the strigillose and piligerous quadrupeds
24 were in a process of excoriation, and others subject to a
25 depilatory, eventeration, or evisceration, and trutination, or
26 ponderation.

sagebrush brook   the west

inclined to write   obliging

1
2 itch for writing   demand   writing desk materials
3 describe in full detail
4 luxurious marriage feast   attendant   very important
5 results
6 trading
7 western   chief city   afternoon
8 village
9 approached   lodging house   attractive
10 pleasing
11 things belonging
12 cleansing   servants   fine farm
13 busily   cautious   careful
14 examining   rear
15 building   beheld
16 bloody   killing
17 fowls   beheadings   calves   sheep
18 curly tailed pigs   hairy
19 wooly   drawing out
20 blood   feathered   winged
21 "two footed"   depriving of feathers
22 coverings   plucking
23 bristly   hairy
24 skinning
25 hair removing process   disemboweling   weighing
26

1   The propinquity of theses operations to my visual
2 powers, evocated in me the conviction that an epulation
3 was approximating; and being somewhat scrutinous and
4 inquisitive, I received cognoscence that on the proximate
5 day a sponsal epulation was to occur.
6   In confabulation with the homiletical and hospitable
7 host antecedent to couchee, Fritz and he produced, in the
8 progress of their enterparlance, mutual and indubious
9 genealogical apodixis, that they stood in relation of cater
10 cousins to each other. In consequence of his great seniority
11 to Fritz, and his early emigration from home, they had
12 anterior to that evening been in a state of nescience to each
13 other.
14   Our concinnity of abearance, and his great comity
15 and xenodochy, as well as his consanguinity to Fritz,
16 educed from him an invitation to us to participate in the
17 hilarity of the approaching nuptials.
18   The parties to be concatenated were his senior
19 daughter and a rurigenous gent of the visue.
20   On the nuptial day, at the horal designation, the
21 guests arrived at the mansion, in wains, curricles, and other
22 vehiculary voitures; upon montures, yawds, plugs,
23 bronchos[8], burros, and equine hybrids with abnormally
24 elongated auricular appendages. There were, also,
25 multitudinous pedestrians.
26   The puisne folk of both genders exhibited
27 themselves in the optimity of their attire.
28   Ultimately the ecclesiastic who was to colligate the
29 parties indissoluble conjugium with the infrangible gyves
30 of Hymen, arrived.
31   He was an octogenarian. His sable envelopes; his
32 lugubrious countenance; the rugosity of his visnomy; his
33 depilous cranium; the rotundity of his person; the gracility
34 of his crural organs; and his ampulliform olfactor, engaged
35 my optics exceedingly.

1 nearness   eyes
2 called forth   feast
3 near at hand   prying
4 inquiring   information   next
5 wedding-feast
6 conversation   talkative   entertaining
7 prior to bedtime
8 conversation   undoubted
9 family descent   proof
10 distant relatives   greater age
11 moving out
12 prior   ignorance
13
14 agreeableness   manners   civilit
15 hospitality   kinship
16 brought forth
17 merriment   wedding
18 united   oldest
19 country born   village
20 wedding   appointed-hour
21 wagons   buggies
22 carriage-conveyances   saddle horses   ordinary horses   jades
23 Mexican ponies   donkeys   horse kind cross-unusually-
24 long-ears, i.e. mules
25 many walkers
26 young
27 very best
28 preacher   bind
29 perpetually binding-marriage tie   inseparable-fetters
30 god of marriage
31 eighty years old   dark clothes
32 solemn   wrinkledness   face
33 bald head   roundness   slenderness
34 legs   bottle shaped nose
35 eyes

1   He coalesced the interests of the amorous pair by
2 confarreation, and immediately after the espousals,
3 anacamtic tintinnabulations from the refectory department,
4 announced a change in the programme. In a brevity of time,
5 the doors of the refectory were made patulous, and the
6 mensal board, onerated with prog, cates, succates, and, in
7 verity, a superabundance of omnifarious cibarious
8 comestibles, displayed itself to dazzled eyes and esurient
9 maws. This mensal structure was soon environed by carls,
10 chuffs, clodpates, clumps, coggers, galliards, rancheros,
11 vaqueros, tauromachians, hoidens, hunks, noodles,
12 dicacious citesses, abigails, oppidans, rustics, verecundious
13 bonnibels, bonnilasses, floricomous whitingmops,
14 pickthanks, poltroons, rantipoles, terreculturists, skipjacks,
15 tosspots, senoritas, bas bleus, and erubescent misses of
16 ineffable pulchritude.
17   So soon as a rogation for a benison by the
18 concionator, transpired, fourchettes, and all implements for
19 the transportation of prog from the table to oral apertures,
20 were movent and sonorific. Such abligurition; such
21 lycanthropic edacity, lurcation, ingurgitation and gulosity;
22 such omnivorousness and pantophagy; and such a mutation
23 and avolation of comestibles, had never fallen under my
24 vision in any antecedent part of my sublunary entity. Truly,
25 anamnestic of Byron's "dura illia messorum!"
26   The fabaceous and other esculent supplies had
27 undergone thorough elixation. The supernaculum and other
28 poculent liquids had been well edulcorated. The
29 gallimaufries, ollapodrida, ragouts, and salmagundi, were
30 all well condited, and were delectable; giving quite an
31 acuity to the gusto of the eaters.
32   After the epigastrics of all had been duly quated,
33 and the appurtenances of the mensal board had been
34 removed, an epithalamium and other ariettas and
35 chansonnettes were chanted by the junior portion of the
36 convivialists. This part of the programme was

1 united   loving couple
2 Roman mode of marriage   marriage
3 resounding   bell ringing   dining room
4 shortness
5 dining hall   thrown open
6 table   loaded   general collection of food
7 fact   more than necessary   all kinds   eatable
8 food   hungry-stomachs
9 table   surrounding   toughs
10 clowns, blockheads, clumsy fellows, sharpers,gay men,ranchmen
11 herdsmen, bull fighters, romps, misers, simpletons
12 talkative city ladies, waiting maids, townsmen, country folks,
13 modest belles, pretty girls, flower bedecked fair lasses
14 officious persons, cowards, rakes, farmers, upstarts
15 topers, beauties, blue stockings   blushing
16 indescribable beauty
17 asking   blessing
18 preacher   table forks
19 food   mouths
20 noisy   prodigal expense for food
21 wolfish greediness   swallowing   gorging   gluttony
22 eating any and every thing   changing
23 flying away   eatables
24 former   life beneath the moon
25 a reminder   "O, ye 'tough insides' of reapers."
26 bean kind   food
27 boiling   fine wine
28 drinks   sweetened
29 hashes   hotchpotch   olio   stewed meats-medley-potpourri
30 seasoned   delightful
31 keenness   appetite
32 stomachs   fully satisfied
33 things belonging   table
34 marriage song
35 merry song
36 merry make

1 unceremoniously interrupted by an uproarous callithumpian
2 charivari by an omniumgatherum rabblement of the
3 vicinage.
4   We all then took consession in a spacious aularian
5 saloon. Fritz and I were soon the cynosures and objects of
6 their oeliads, as peregrine aliens in their midst. I saw them
7 nictate and susurrate, and they seemed much titillated at our
8 neoteric appearance among them. We, however,
9 disregarded their abderian ludifications. When the parson
10 had withdrawn, they inchoated saltation, which some
11 performed with considerable legerity; especially, the
12 presultor.
13   Those of the feminine gender, appeared in the
14 optimity of their attractions. The tetes of some had
15 undergone much unique and artistic capillature; and the
16 capital crinitory filaments of others had been so crispated
17 by the instruments of tonsorial friseurs, as to resemble the
18 spiral flexures of the caudal extremity of a porcine
19 quadruped. Their chapeaus were gorgeously plumed, and
20 hyperbolically and fulgidly ornated. Their sericeous
21 fazzolets and bombycinous mokadours were brilliant and
22 highly odorated. Their faces had been rubricated and
23 infucated with fucus. Indeed they exhibited such flirtation
24 that almost affected me with misogyny.
25   Fritz and I exhilarated a knot of guests with orphean
26 strains upon the guimbard; and with bon mots, quips, and
27 rebuses; and rendered other auxiliations, to the best of our
28 appropriaments; but we did not tripudiate, or participate in
29 any gallimatias.
30   When all had received satiation as to the diversified
31 amusements, especially, terpsichorean indulgence, the
32 coterie disbanded. At one time, all were hugely
33 conquassated by the diffusion of some pulverized
34 mundungus on the floor.
35   I indulged in a permansion with Fritz's complaisant
36 and harberous german for the diuternity of a fortnight.

1 very noisy
2 mock serenade   general gathering of common people
3 villages
4 sitting together   roomy hall
5 centre of attraction
6 side glances   strange   foreigners
7 wink   whisper   amused
8 recent
9 giggling   fun making
10 began   dancing
11 nimbleness
12 leader of the dance
13
14 very best   wigs
15 nothing like it   ingenious   frizzing
16 hair of the head   curled
17 barber-hair dressers
18 winding curls   pig's tails
19 hats   showily adorned with bright feathers
20 exaggeratedly and brilliantly ornamented   silken
21 handkerchiefs
22 perfumed   stained reddened
23 face paint
24 woman hatred
25 entertained
26 entrancing music   jews' harp   smart sayings   jokes
27 riddles   assistance
28 abilities   dance
29 foolishness
30 satisfaction
31 various   dancing
32 gathering
33 shaken up
34 powdered tobacco
35 stay   genial
36 hospitable   kinsman   duration   week

1 During this tarriance, I witnessed much of very momentous
2 import.
3   The nimiety and superalimentation of multifarious
4 cibarious substances engorged into inane and jejune
5 stomachs during the nuptial festivity , were extremely
6 nosopoetic, and some of the guests were ferried,-nolens
7 volens,-by Charon, over the river Styx.
8   The morbific character of the maladies became
9 manifest variously in their physical organization. Some
10 were seized with deuteropathy; some with ephialtes; others
11 with apepsy, emesis, megrim, epistaxis, or sanguineous
12 manations from their nasal orifices; some were affected
13 with gingival and hepatical intumescence and lippitude;
14 others were beset with catalepsis, subitaneous lypothymy,
15 succeeded by subsultory exagitations; in others were
16 generated dyspnœa, aglutition, distension of the
17 pericardium and pneumonia, induced by saltation and
18 inhalation of pulverized nicotian.
19   Couriers were ablegated from all parts of the villatic
20 community to secure adjuments of pharmacopolists
21 chirurgeons, physicians, and even Hobson's choice
22 charlatans and amethodists.
23   In their diagnostications and prognostications, and
24 their discovering procatarctic causes, and prescribing, there
25 was no consimilitude. Not all of them were professionally
26 versed and skilled in materia medica, and the medical and
27 surgical departments of pathology; – nosology, ætiology,
28 morbid anatomy, symptomatology, and therapeutics; and as
29 a sequence, some of them shot wide of the mark as to
30 pathognomic symptoms.
31   When I brought my zetetic æsculapian battery to
32 bear upon one of them, I discovered he could not
33 differentiate among maladies – epidemic, endemic and
34 sporadic; infections and contagious.
35   The one who officiated in the vicinity of the
36 hacienda, imparted the following pharmaceutical recipes: –

1 stay   great importance
2
3 excess   overeating   various
4 food   empty   craving
5 marriage
6 unwholesome   willing or unwilling
7 ferryman at river Styx   river in the lower world
8 disease producing   ailments
9 evident   bodies
10 headache from overloaded stomach   nightmare
11 indigestion   vomiting   nervous   headache
12 nose bleeding
13 inflammation of gums and liver   sore eyes
14 fits   sudden   fainting
15 jerking agitations
16 difficulty in breathing and swallowing
17 heart sac   inflammation of lungs   dancing
18 powdered tobacco
19 sent out   village
20 aid   druggist
21 surgeons   doctors   that or none
22 quacks and imposters
23 recognizing symptoms present and future
24 exciting causes
25 similarity
26 practice of medicine
27 science of diseases   classification   cause
28 organic changes   symptoms and cure   result
29
30 characteristics of disease
31 inquiring   medical
32
33 explain the different diseases   wide spreading   local
34 few and scattering   from the air   contact
35
36 farm   prescriptions

1 For megrim and lippitude, – acupuncturation, and
2 scarification on the cutaneous integument of the cranium;
3 for lypothymy, the extravasation of the rubric fluid by
4 venesection, or phlebotomy; for subsultory exagitations, a
5 sudatory diaphoretics, and hypnotics; for nasal hemorrhage,
6 styptics applied to the rhinal emunctory; for
7 imposthumation, – argillaceous illutations; for ephialtes,
8 apepsy, and deuteropathy, – antephialtitics,
9 Baunscheidtism, and calefacient sinapisms; for illiac
10 disquietudes, – stingo immixed with ginger and cayenne
11 pepper; for aglutition, or dysphagy, – œsophagotomy; for
12 dyspnoea, – bronchotomy, or pharyngotomy.
13   Should all these fail, or prove inutile, he insisted on
14 an adhibition, as a succedaneum and adjuvant, of an
15 apozem, or excoction of hederaceous and other radicals and
16 corticals, which, depurated of lees by percolation, or
17 transcolation, and well dulcorated, would lose its
18 injucundity and become totally innocuous. With this
19 apozemical treatment should be connected eccritics, or
20 drastic deobstruents and emetics. Ingeminations of very
21 calefacient epispastics, and copious phlebotomy should be
22 sedulously protracted until the invaletudinarian became
23 almost exsanguinous and evanid, anæmic and thanatold –
24 autoptically exanimate. Should a patient, from sudations,
25 venesections, vesicants, and other cutaneous appliances,
26 become sweltry, adhibitions of aqueous aspersions upon the
27 epidermis, should be sedulously secured.
28   He asseverated that these medicamental appliances
29 would have the most salutiferous syndrome; and that after
30 an imminution of the patient's obesity by strict
31 limotherapeia, his abstersed, emaciated, and adynamic
32 system might be instaurated with cardiacs and peptic
33 sauces. He iterated the assertion that from his proficiency in
34 angiography, anthropology, pharmacodynamics,
35 threpsology, therapeutics and prophylactics, he knew the

1 headache and sore eyes   needle puncturing
2 scratching with sharp instrument, skin covering of the head
3 for swooning   letting out the blood
4 vein cutting   bleeding   convulsions
5 sweat perspiration and sleep producers   nose bleeding
6 astringents   nose
7 abscesses   clay poultices   for nightmare
8 indigestion and headache   nightmare remedies
9 rubbing cure   very hot blistering plasters   bowel
10 troubles   very strong liquor
11 difficult swallowing   cutting the throat
12 difficult breathing   cutting the windpipe
13 fail in right effect
14 application   substitute   helper
15 tea   decoction   ivy   roots
16 barks   purified   dregs   filtering
17 straining   sweetened
18 disagreeableness   altogether harmless
19 tea   medicines to promote discharges
20 powerful purgatives and emetics   repetitions
21 hot mustard plasters   abundant bleeding
22 persistently continued   patient
23 bloodless   faint   very weak   death like
24 apparently lifeless   perspirations
25 bloodletting   blistering   skin
26 oppressed with heat   applications   water sprinkling
27 outer skin   industriously
28 declared   medical
29 health producing course
30 decrease   fleshiness
31 fasting   cleansed   lean   debilitated
32 restored   strengthening medicines   digestives
33 repeated   thorough knowledge of the
34 blood vessels of man   the effects of drugs
35 science of nutrition, cure and primary causes of diseases

1 employment of this medicamental treatment would make
2 sanation certain.
3   He impignorated his veracity that the patient would
4 be invested with an almost immarcessible floriage; and
5 that, in his supputation with them, he would not be
6 scrupulously exacting as to lucrific guerdon. In diametrical
7 oppugnance to his æsculapian skill and the remedial
8 treatment with diacatholicons, polychrests, and adiaphorous
9 placebos, some of the maladies were mortiferous, and
10 several of the puisne folks were soon irremediably
11 moribund, and made their exit for the irremeable bourne, –
12 Erebus and the realms of sprites.
13   The amethodist's medicamenta were so narcotic and
14 lethiferous, that the victims of his indexterity, in the
15 ultimity of their terrestrial vitality, were favored with
16 euthanasy.
17   The hilarity of the nuptial epulation merged into
18 lugubrious aspects. Resplendent habiliments were
19 succeeded by sable paraphernalia of obsequies; and the
20 cantata of jovialities were followed by exequial arvals and
21 epicedian threnodes. And O, the cadent lachrymary
22 effusions of the clonic and clamant ging!
23   The medicus commingled with the suspiring
24 threnetic throng in the procession to the necropolis for the
25 inhumation of the decedents; but notwithstanding his
26 fletiferous crocodility, he maintained the most astounding
27 adiophory and ataraxy.
28   Subsequent to the sepelition of the reliquiæ, he
29 exhibited his carte blanche, variegated with multitudinous
30 numerical additaments; – most ocularly indicant of his
31 questuary, coetous, and covinous proclivities. After
32 impleting his nummary receptacle, he made his disparition.
33   Most veritably and lexicographically,
34   Ihr freund,
35   Ivan

1 medical
2 restoration to health
3 pledged truthfulness
4 unfading bloom of youth
5 settlement
6 particularly paying recompense direct
7 opposition healing
8 universal remedies harmless prescriptions
9 only to please mortal
10 younger beyond remedies
11 at death's door departure returnless goal
12 region of the dead kingdom of spirits
13 quack's drugs poisonous
14 fatal
15 last stages life on earth
16 easy death
17 merry making marriage-feast
18 mournful scenes splendid attire
19 dark appendages funeral rites
20 songs of joy funeral feasts
21 funeral songs falling tear outpourings
22 convulsed weeping crowd
23 doctor living mourning company
24 graveyard
25 burial dead
26 affected sorrow
27 indifference calmness
28 after burial bodies
29 blanks with signatures many
30 figures added evidently showing
31 seeking craving dishonest inclinations
32 filling money purse disappearance
33 truly dictionary making
34 [Ger.] Your friend

LETTER VI
Mesquite Boscage, Occident
June 1, 1873

Most bibliophilistical Sir: –

1   In the finale of my primal lexiphanic
2 epistolography, I imparted to you the verity, that femininity
3 had not effacinated me. Not so, however, as to my chum,
4 Fritz. He does not believe that – *amare et sapere vix deo*
5 *conceditur;* – and consequently, he is about to become a
6 neogamist, by being colligated with hymenean fetters. He
7 will doubtless soon be the beatific occupant of his own
8 hacienda, environed by the maximum of paradisiacal
9 subcelestial felicity.
10   Without much circuity, I will give you the
11 concatenation of circumsntances leading to the present
12 status of his amatorial venture, – and imprimis, give you a
13 laconic biographic sketch of Fritz.
14   He was, during his adolescency, a paralian.
15   His ancestral habitation was conterminous to the
16 maritimale sections of this splendrous columbian republic,
17 where the congestion of population and the celsitude of the
18 means for the sustentation of vitality, necessitated those
19 who had, by herculean and invincible difficulties, become
20 depauperated, to emigrate to the untenanted portions of our
21 occidental domain.
22   Often he could not evitate the emission of the most
23 grave suspirations in view of the atrabilarian aspects of his
24 natal vicinity, and of the unswayable approximation of the
25 detorsion from the operatives, of the media of obtaining a
26 competency, by opulent monopolies.

book loving

1 latter part   bombastic letter
2 fact   womankind
3 charmed
4 to love and be wise is scarcely permitted even to a god
5
6 person newly married   bound   marriage shackles
7 happy
8 fine farm   surrounded   greatest   like paradise
9 under heaven   happiness
10 indirectness
11 chain
12 situation   love undertaking   in the first place
13 brief   life history
14 youth   dweller near the sea
15 parental abode   bordering on
16 sea coast   American
17 denseness   highness
18 sustaining life
19 very difficult   incontrollable
20 impoverished   move out   unoccupied
21 western
22 avoid
23 sighs   melancholy
24 native   ungovernable   approach
25 wrenching away   laborers   means
26 livelihood   rich companies controlling trade

1   However sedulous in any avocation, but few could
2 participate in the reception of correspondent remunerative
3 guerdon.
4   The incessant crescive density of the transmontane
5 population impelled the proprietors of terra firma to such
6 constant ingeminate arations and inseminations of their
7 granges for the eduction of radical, herbaceous,
8 leguminous, and frumentarious cerealia, that terrene
9 infecundity, even of the most batful soils, inevitably
10 resulted.
11   Not only so, but the discinding of the granges into
12 exiguous, multangular, and multilateral fragments, made
13 them too angust for occupancy. A mature cogitation upon
14 the accreting congeries of the discommodities in prospect
15 for his natal land, brought him to the acturience to
16 effectuate a segregation of himself from the localities that
17 witnessed the gambols of his juvenility, and procure for
18 himself a domiciliation in the spacious occident. The
19 announcement of this illation imparted a lugubrious phase
20 to the physiognomies of his paternal and maternal, or
21 rather, – novercal, – relations; but illumed risibilities upon
22 the phizes of his enemies.
23   When the doloriferous moment arrived when his
24 discession was to take its inception, his germans, agnations
25 and cognations, in conjunction with many of his vicinal
26 cotemporaries, congregated about him. His parents were
27 loth to behold their entire orbation; and the rest, because his
28 migration subjected them to the amission of an adjuvant
29 neighbor.
30   The edicts of the Fates have been quite propitious to
31 him since his ubiety in the occident.
32   A very pecunious consanguineal avuncular relative,
33 – an agamist, and a nonagenarian, – having terminated his
34 subsolar vitality, bequeathed to Fritz all his terrestrial
35 acquisitions. He has also received his patrimonial

1 persevering   calling
2 paying recompense
3
4 continual growing   beyond the mountains
5 forced   owners   land
6 repeated ploughings   seeding
7 farms   production   roots   herb and
8 bean kind   grain   soil
9 exhaustion   fertile
10
11 cutting up   farms
12 narrow   many cornered   many sided
13 small   full deliberation
14 growing masses   inconveniences
15 native   impulse
16 to act   separation
17 sportive pranks   youth
18 home   roomy west
19 decision   solemn appearance
20 countenances   father   mother
21 stepmother   radiant smiles
22 countenances
23 sad
24 departure   beginning   cousins   relations on father's side
25 mother's side   village
26 associates   collected
27 bereavement
28 going away   loss   helping
29
30 decrees   destiny controllers   favorable
31 presence   west
32 wealthy   blood related   uncle
33 bachelor   ninety years old   ended
34 life beneath the sun   willed   earthly
35 possessions   ancestral

1 cleronomy. The aggregate, which was not inconsiderable,
2 enabled him to effect the emption of a hacienda.
3   The campestrian and horticultural enclosures are
4 very feracious and frugiferous. The manse is palatial. The
5 croft is venust and attractive.
6   Multifarious and multigenerous floriferous,
7 nuciferous, pomiferous, pyriferous, pruniferous, and other
8 fructiferous trees and plantage are not minus. Here he can,
9 unannoyed by bombylious puncturing culices, and other
10 sanguivorous sanguisuges and animalculæ, indulge his
11 ingenerate somnolency, and enjoy superlative otiosity,
12 autocratorically.
13   The interior appurtenances and garniture of his won
14 is unisonous with the exterior aspect, and this educed from
15 him the plerophory that he was still under degarnishment
16 whilst minus a femme d'charge, and unassociated with one
17 of the costal genus. His gynephobia minorated most
18 perceptibly, and his appetition for the spousal state became
19 quite puissant. His erotism impelled him to frequent a
20 nundinal occasion, where, percase, he ogled for the first
21 time, at his prospective cara sposa. He espied her in
22 consociation with a templar, – a politicaster, – whose
23 fatuity and parvanimity was visible in all his abearance.
24   A sagittal puncture through his pericardium effected
25 such a clarity in his optics, that he beheld a millenary of
26 charms in her venust physique. Her roseate labials; her
27 liliaceous cuticle; her graceful locomotive organs; and her
28 mellifluent and suaviloquent loquacity, most parlously
29 enamored him, and divested him of all autarchy.
30   Having effected an enterparlance with her, he found
31 spontaneity of interlocution to be mutual; for the erotic
32 arcubalister had arctuated his ballister and jaculated a
33 sagittary vire into her cordialities also; but the eviction of
34 the templar from her companionship was the punctilio of
35 his mental perturbations. This quodlibet induced upon him
36 the most labefying anorexy and erotomy; but having a

1 inheritance   sum total
2 purchase   fine farm
3 filed and garden
4 fertile   fruitful   dwelling house   magnificent
5 adjoining grounds   beautiful
6 many kinds and varieties of flower
7 nut   apple   pear   plum
8 and other fruit bearing   wanting
9 buzzing   piercing   mosquitoes
10 blood devouring   blood suckers   insects
11 inborn   inclination to sleep   greatest ease
12 with absolute impunity
13 belongings   adornment   house
14 in unison   brought forth
15 full persuasion   lack of furnishments
16 lacking   housekeeper
17 rib kind   dread of women   lessened
18 desire   married
19 powerful   love fit
20 fair   perhaps   cast sheep's eyes
21 spouse
22 company   law student   would be politician
23 stupidity   little mindedness   behavior
24 arrow perforation   heart sac
25 clearness   eyes   thousand
26 beautiful form   rosy lips
27 lily like skin   walking
28 sweet   persuasive   talkativeness   dangerously
29 captivated   robbed   self control
30 interview
31 unrestrained   voluntary conversation
32 love shooter   bent-cross bow   hurled
33 barbed arrow   affections   getting rid of
34 lawyer   difficult question
35 mind disturbance   problem
36 weakening   loss of appetite   love sickness

1 prevision that the politicaster's debonairness to her was
2 rather impermanent, he brought him into proximity with a
3 linguacious, psychagogical citess, which effected a
4 detraction of all his antecedaneous comity to Miss
5 Amenity. Having thus segregated the macaroni from her
6 society, he – making me his privado, and enlisting my
7 auxiliary adjuvancy, – dispatched to her a billet d'amour
8 somewhat after the following diction and phraseology: –
9
10 Alderliefest and most debonair Miss; –
11   Desiderating not to be ambagitory in the prolegomenary
12 part of this epistle, and waiving all supervacaneous
13 apologies, I will announce to you that I have a proclivity to
14 assume the marital state, and that, since our recent tete a tete
15 interlocution, I have delapsed into a dilection which has
16 elicited this amatory epistolography to you, and extorted the
17 conviction that you are the rara avis in consortion with him
18 the suavities and amaritudes of my subastral vitality might
19 be felicitously sustained. Ergo, my prelation of you, and my
20 optation to impart to you a categorical catenation of the
21 prerequisites, assuetudes, and habilitations of her in whose
22 sodality I am to protract my subcelestial career in this
23 asperous and subdolous megacosm to the time of my obit.
24   Primarily, her physical structure must be staminal
25 and sane. She must not be a lilliputian, nor of more than
26 medial procerity; neither osseous, nor encumbered with a
27 superabundance of adipous tissue. Her physique must be
28 venust, and her physiognomy bonny and nitid as Phosphor
29 herself. Her articulations must be as mellifluent and
30 euphonious as those of the rosignol. Her ambulations must
31 be perk and facile. She must never us fucus nor prink. She
32 must adonize herself, but never envelope herself in
33 sericeuos, or bombycinous habiliments and glittering
34 arraiment, except on ecclesiastical, nundinary, and ferial
35 occasions. She must not be circumforaneous, nor
36 multiloquous; and never become a quidnunc. Never be

1 foresight   politeness
2 temporary   contact
3 talkative   attractive city lady
4 withdrawal   former polite attentions
5 separated   fop
6 confidante
7 assistance   love letter
8 language and sentence structure
9
10 best beloved   courteous
11 desiring   indirect   introductory
12 letter   omitting   useless
13 inclination
14 married   face to face
15 conversation   fallen   love
16 brought forth   love letter   forced
17 model person   companionship
18 sweets and bitters   life beneath the stars
19 happily   therefore   preference
20 great desire   absolute   chain
21 first requirements   customs   habits
22 society   under heaven
23 rough   treacherous   great world   death
24 first place   body   stout
25 sound   dwarf very small
26 medium height   bony
27 too much   fatness   form
28 beautiful   face   cheerful   bright   Venus
29 sweetly flowing
30 harmonious   nightingale   walking
31 quick   graceful   face paint   dress for show
32 beautify
33 silk attire
34 church   fair   holiday
35 going from house to house
36 gadding   news monger

1 dowdyish nor procacious. She must exhibit idoneous
2 pudicity and obmutescence in the presence of frens.
3 She must be au fait in the usance of euphemisms, and
4 never divulge huggermuggers.
5 The evitation of saponaceous abstergents and other
6 mundifying media to oviate somatic fetidness, and a
7 premature rugose phiz, and apparent anility, must never
8 denote her. She must possess interminable longanimity, and
9 never affect any deliquium in any subitaneous fright.
10 Fumigation, ructation, and immoderate yexing, and
11 oscitancy, must not be indulged in, in my presence.
12 She must be skilled in domiculture, and in such
13 hariolation as aleuromancy, myomancy, pyromancy,
14 capnomancy, and enoptomancy; dextrous in panification,
15 and in the preparation of polygenous and polymorphous
16 refections; habile in malaxation, and the facture of cakes of
17 brank and other cerealia; adept in the confection of cates,
18 juncates, simnels, succates, and in verity, scient and perite in
19 the facture of omnigen ous comestibles in the culinary
20 department. Eke, she must be well versed as to the chemical
21 constituents of smegmatic substances, and exhibit
22 solertiousness in manufacturing same; and at times operate
23 the filatory. She must not be unduly affected with
24 anthomania, but instead, occupy her leisure time in
25 interbastation; and be not to orgillous to superintend the
26 incubation of gallinaceous autophagi, and impart to their
27 lanuginous and vociferous progeny ample saginating
28 nutrication.
29 To all murine quadrupeds, and all vermiparous, pulicous,
30 and culiciform multipeds, and animalculæ, and to all
31 sanguivorous thoral cimisses about the premises, she must be
32 ruthlessly lethiferous.
33 She must inhibit all unnecessary perstreperous boations
34 and clamations among the dandiprats, and sedulously
35 urbanize all the abigails, and all the ancillaries and factotums
36 under her suvranty.

1 vulgar looking   petulant
2 proper modesty   silence   strangers
3 expert   use of pleasant sayings
4 family secrets
5 avoidance   soap cleansers
6 purifying means   avoid bodily offensive odor
7 too early wrinkled face   old womanhood
8 characterize   unending patience
9 swooning   sudden
10 smoking   belching   excessive hiccoughing
11 gaping
12 housekeeping
13 foretelling from flour, mice, fire,
14 smoke and mirrors   bread making
15 all kinds and forms
16 bakery   skillful   kneading dough   making
17 buckwheat   grain   dainty or choice foods[9]
18 crisp breads   fact   learned and expert
19 all kinds of food   kitchen
20 moreover
21 ingredients   soap
22 show skill
23 work at the spinning wheel
24 fondness for flowers
25 quilting   proud
26 hatching   domestic fowls
27 downy   noisy   offspring   abundant   fattening
28 nourishment
29 mice   worms   fleas
30 flies   insects
31 blood devouring bedbugs
32 unmercifully death dealing
33 forbid   boisterous   noise
34 crying   children   diligently
35 make polite   waiting maids   maid servants   roustabouts
36 control

1   In fine, she must be panurgic, and know that I am an
2 absolutistic acephalist in my own domicile. I am favorable to
3 a synarchy or a diarchy, but diametrically contrariant and
4 antagonistic to all gynecocracy.
5   I have a prenotion that the antecedent enumerated
6 aggregation of physical, ethical, and economical
7 habilitations have a more spacious depository in you than in
8 any other of your gender that has fallen under my vision; and
9 in view of it, I tender to you for your acceptance, the cincture
10 of Hymen.
11   In perclose, if you can reciprocate the eupathy which
12 idited this amatory epistolographical effusion, a favorable
13 replication will most veritably, invest me with inenarrable
14 delectation.
15
16   With metreless amity,
17   Most erotically, yours,
18   Fritz.
19
20 A response, as follows, was accorded.
21
22   Most suasory Sir: –
23
24   I am the accipient of your most inopinate complimentary
25 erotic epistle.
26   Posterior to a careful lection and perpension of its
27 momental import, which greatly perturbed my accustomary
28 somnolency, I now, having my medium serenitude,
29 alacriously impart to you a response.
30   I am still celibate, though having arrived at the age of
31 muliebrity, and hence, nubile for several annuary epochs. I
32 have had multitudinous allectations to enter into a maritated
33 state, but I have, as yet, evitated all morsure at the
34 inescations coming from your gender: and all illaqueations,
35 and all illecebrous subarrations from adcaptandum
36 amorosos. Whatever might evene, I have been

1 cunning in all kinds of work and business
2 absolute acknowledger of no superior   house
3 joint rule   government by two   directly adverse and opposed
4 woman rule
5 foreknowledge   foregoing   mentioned
6 assemblage   bodily   moral   business
7 qualifications   roomy lodgment
8
9 girdle
10 of the god of marriage
11 conclusion   make return for   good feeling
12 prompted   love letter   outpouring
13 reply   truly   indescribable
14 delight
15
16 measureless love
17 greatly in love
18
19
20
21
22 persuasive
23
24 unexpected
25 love letter
26 after   reading   considering
27 great importance   disturbed
28 usual drowsiness   quietude
29 cheerfully
30 unmarried
31 womanhood   marriageable   years
32 many enticements   married
33 avoided   biting
34 baits   set snares
35 alluring betrothal gifts   catch favor lovers
36 happen

1	procinct against a procidence to a state of deterioration by
2	an infrangible consortion with petit-maitres, or jackanapes
3	in fulgid ornature, and hyperbolical, pavonian arraiment.
4	Such could never enter the cycle of my recognized
5	amorists.
6	Festination by many of my sex to an inextricable
7	sponsal colligation with such mangonized quidams and
8	asinegos, has crebrously obnubilated the most lucent
9	prospicience of aleger juvenility. Such eventuations made
10	me meticulous, and by no means, proclive to adjugate my
11	mundane allotment to any goman, or animal implumes
12	biped. I came almost to the illation to become a
13	Malthusian; at least, to be solivagant through this
14	multivious megacosm to my ulterior requietory.
15	Since our tete a tete collocution in the manse of the
16	amicable aubergist, during nundinal occasion, I have had
17	an ineffable propendency for your society. Moreover,
18	your sapiential epistle caused a bannition of all
19	equilibration from my lacerated petto, and premonstrated
20	to me that you are, by no means, an agrammatist, but in
21	verity, a sapient belletristical philomath.
22	You were not wholly ignote to me prior to my primal
23	vision of you at our adventive meeting and confabulation.
24	Your heliograph had already fallen under my vision, and
25	caused me to cherish a preexistimation for you.
26	However, in my cogitations as to the prerequisites,
27	and characteristic qualifications of him who may wish to
28	be my marital comate, I have formulated the following; –
29	Primarily, he must be a franklin, or yeoman, though
30	not an amnicolist. His agrestical mansion must have a
31	roborous contignation, glabrous floors, multiudinous[10]
32	fenestral apertures, an imposing exedra, or antesolarium,
33	various vestiaries, and a balneary. It must be well
34	camerated, and impervious to the hyperborean frigefactive
35	perflations of the Aquilon. It must be environed by ample

1 prepared   degradation   inferiorit
2 inseparable companionship   insignificant lovers   fops
3 dazzling   decorations   exaggerated   peacock attire
4 circle
5 lovers
6 haste
7 marriage bond   dressed to catch favor   nobody knows who
8 blockheads   often clouded   brightest
9 prospects   cheerful youth   consequences
10 timid   inclined   yoke
11 earthly career   husband   Plato's man [two legged animal
12 without feathers]   conclusion
13 believer in checking increase in population   lone wanderer
14 full of reads   great world   last resting place
15 face to face conversation   home
16 friendly innkeeper   fair
17 unspeakable proneness
18 full of wisdom letter   banishment
19 equal balance   turn up breast   foreshown
20 illiterate
21 fact   wise   well read   lover of learning
22 unknown previous   first view
23 accidental   conversation
24 photograph
25 previous esteem
26 deliberations   prime requirements
27 peculiar endowments
28 spousal associate
29 in the first place   land owner
30 dweller near a river   country residence
31 strong framework   smooth   many
32 windows   attractive   balcony and portico
33 wardrobes   bathroom
34 ceiled   proof against   very cold freezing
35 blasts   North wind   surrounding

1 avenues, covered with scorbiform and arenaceous
2 material. A gelid puit must not be minus.
3 　　The housal furnishments must be of medium
4 preciosity. In the culinary department, adeps, farinaceous,
5 lactaceous, ovicular, and saccharine substances for the
6 facture of omnigenous doucets, simnels, and omnifarious
7 pannary comestibles, must not be wanting. Flabels,
8 locofocos, or allumettes, and sebaceous and kerosene
9 luciferous lucerns, and other nocturnal illuminators must
10 be in abundance.
11 　　The ecuries and the byres, as also their environs, must
12 exuberate in montures, and other equines; also,
13 multitudinous bovine, vaccine, vituline, lanigerous ovine,
14 and porcine, or suilline, quadrupeds; all in a state of
15 rotund impinguation, or sagination. Reciprocornous
16 arietating malodorous hircines will not be tolerated.
17 　　The corporeal structure of him who is to be my
18 comate, must not be too procere; – at least, he must not be
19 a brobdignagian, – and by no means, must he be a
20 homunculus. Not too rotund nor too angular. He must be
21 equicrural, and not macropodous or claudicant; not
22 macrognathic or macrotous; and somewhat
23 macrencephalous. In verity, his physique must be
24 adonean.
25 　　He must be very deft in his arraiment, and keep his
26 labials mundified from all nicotian succulence; – in verity,
27 sedulously evitate, at all times, the manducation,
28 ebolition, and nasal inhalation of the noxious plantage. He
29 must not be an œnophilist, but a very abstemious
30 nephalist. He must evitate disassiduity as to the
31 mundification of his dental organs, and cutaneous surface.
32 He must never be desidious in pediluvy, balneation, and
33 salination, for the remotion of hogo, occasioned by
34 exsudations, and dermal desquamations. During a
35 procellous and lutarious season, he must sedulously
36 absterge all illutation from his pedial extremities, prior to
37 making his introgression to the house.

1 walks   sawdust   sandy
2 cold spring   lacking
3 house furniture
4 costliness   kitchen   lard   flour
5 milk   eggs   sugar
6 making all kinds   custards   cracknels   various kinds
7 bread   eatables
8 fans   friction matches   wax   coal oil
9 light giving   lamps   night light givers
10
11 stables   cow houses   surroundings
12 abound   saddle horses   horse stock
13 many oxen   cows   calves   wool bearing sheep
14 hogs   swine
15 round plumpness   fatness   crooked horned butting
16 bad smelling goats   endured
17 bodily form
18 associate   tall
19 giant
20 dwarf   pursy fat   lean and lank
21 equal legged   big footed   lame
22 long jawed   big eared
23 large headed   fact   form
24 perfection of beauty
25 ingenious   clothing
26 lips cleansed   tobacco juice   ambier   fact
27 persistently avoid   chewing
28 smoking   breathing through nose   pernicious
29 wine drinker   total abstainer
30 avoid want of care
31 purifying   teeth   skin
32 negligent   feet washing   bathing
33 salt water baths   riddance   disagreeable odor
34 perspirations   scarf skin scaling
35 rainy   muddy   industriously
36 cleanse   mud coatings   feet
37 entering

Sputation on the tapis will not be tolerated, and the
nonessential augean cuspidor must be – non est.

All mussitation relative to the elixation and
preparation of cibarious articles of alimentation, are
peremptorily tabooed.

In company, he must be bonnair and homiletic; and
never querulential, or of too potestative portance. In his
collocution, he must be a quodlibetarian, but not a
monologist; and by no means, pompatic, umbratious,
temerarious, clerkless, or incony; devoid of all
incivism, inertitude, perfunctoriness, and ingannation.
He must not be a punctilious precisianist; never too
captious, and scoptically nasute; never guilty of
macrology, psilology, balbucination, or heterophemy.

By no means, must he be stertorous in his
obdormition, or be subject to somniloquism and
somnambulism. In his operosity in this subcelestial
arena, he must not be a mammonite, or be given to
cosmolatry. He must be very homiletical and altruistic
towards eleemosynaries, inmates of orphanotrophies,
sportularies, and those in a state of obolary viduity.

Adunation with any of the existential cryptic
germanities, or guilds, and all noctivagations, and
omnivagations, subjecting me to solitariety, and
solicitous excubations, must never characterize him.
Indiscriminate fidejussion must never have
immancency in his harns. An abjurement of all
miscreance and demonocracy and demonolatry; and a
cordial acceptation of Christianity, must ever denote
him.

He must be lusory with the bairns, and
paradigmatical to them; and indulge them freely in their
anthromorphized feats of equestrianism and sciomachy,
and in their barmecidal sybaritic feasts; and erudiate
and indoctrinate them to be veridical, without baculine
vapulation, or fustigation.

1 spitting   carpet
2 filthy   spittoon   not present
3 fussing   cooking
4 edible   nutriment
5 forbidden
6 polite   entertaining
7 quarrelsome   authoritative
8 conversation   learned on all subjects
9 one who does all the talking   vain   easily endangered
10 headstrong   unbusiness like   impolite   free from
11 rudeness   laziness   carelessness   deception
12 exactingly precise
13 faultfinding   jokingly smart
14 talking too much,talking nonsense,stammering,saying what
15 is not meant   snoring
16 sleep   talking in sleep
17 sleep walking   labors   under heaven
18 sphere of action   money worshipper
19 world worship   obliging   unselfish
20 those living on charity   orphan homes
21 those living on alms   moneyless widowhood
22 uniting   existing secret societies
23 organizations   night roving
24 rambling   loneliness
25 sitting up late
26 general going surety
27 indwelling   brain   renunciation
28 false religion   superstition   demon worship
29
30
31 playful   children
32 set model example   humor
33 mimicking grown people   horsemanship   sham battles
34 imaginary luxurious banquets   teach
35 instruct   truthful   rod punishment
36 cudgeling

The sponsal munities I claim for myself, are: – To be autocratix in all departments of the domicile, and assume full solidarity-alibi,-algates. Consent for protracted evagations, and obequitations, when desiderated, must be alacriously granted. All seminations, aberuncations, and sarculations in the hortulan sepiment; the pabulation of vaccine, equine, and curvicaudate procine quadrupeds; and the ablactation of the mugient vituline quadrupeds; and in verity, all latreutical work about the equerry, the vaccary, and the lactary, is most explicitly recused.

In case the omega of my sponsal partner should antedate mine, impignoration not to enjoy digamy, or deuterogamy, will not be given, in my desponsation to any adamite, or masculine biped of the genus homo. Should a catalysis of the sponsal affiliation evene, – and that by diffarreation, on account of inebriety, or any other malefaction, then, a dimidiation of the acquisitions would have to occur.

Finally, should my mari and I enjoy consenescence, and be nearly commorient, and my obital period antevene his, then my desideration is, to be funerated debonairly in a feateous requietory. Such are the munities I reserve for myself, and to which I surmise you will readily yield assentment. Your supravulgar cogitations, as well as your position beyond the purlieus of plebeiance must lucidly premonstrate it.

On condition of compliance with the above requisitions, I accept your proffered cincture of Hymen, with the esperance that our connubial adunation and consequent solidarity and interdependency may cause an amelioration of the asperities incident to our terrestrial vitality, and aid us in the devitation of many of the tentations in this immund and inquinated mundane structure; and I leave it to your arbitrament to designate the day of bridality. Perchance the proximate plenilune would be the most idoneous period for the hymeneal conjugation; and may the supermundane powers

1 marriage rights   above earth
2 absolute mistress
3 equal rights and authority elsewhere   everywhere
4 excursions   horseback outings   desired
5 cheerfully   seed sowing   grubbing
6 weeding   garden   feeding
7 cows   horses   curly tailed pigs
8 weaning   bawling calves
9 fact   servile   stables
10 cow house   dairy   declined
11 death   husband
12 happen before   pledging   second marriage
13 betrothment
14 son of Adam   humankind
15 dissolution   wedlock association occur
16 divorce   drunkenness
17 evil doing   division   property
18
19 husband   growing old together
20 dying at the same time   decease   come before
21 desire   buried nicely
22 beautiful   resting place   rights
23 believe
24 agreement   above vulgar thoughts
25 outskirts   lower classes   clearly
26 foreshow
27
28 girdle of god of marriage
29 hope   matrimonial union
30 union of interests   mutual dependence
31 making better   roughness   earthly
32 life   shunning
33 temptations   unclean   polluted   world
34 decision
35 marriage union   perhaps   next full moon
36 suitable   wedding

1   invest the paranymphal occasion with their auspicious
2   benison.
3   In an aureate ligature,
4   Your eviternal affianced,
5   E.M. Amenity.
6
7   Fritz has given me assecuration that the said
8 paranymphal occasion will occur as suggested, and not on
9 the Greek calends. However, as to the culmination and final
10 sequel, – more anon.
11   I will now bring to a finis this sesquipedalian
12 cacographical scrawl, with the assurance that
13   I am,
14   Yours, pedantically,
15   Ivan

1 Dignify marriage favorable
2 blessing
3 golden band
4 forever in plighted faith
5
6
7 assurance
8 nuptial
9 not at all, as the Greeks had no calends turning point
10 result
11 close long worded
12 badly written
13
14 school master like

LETTER VII
Megalopolis of the Occident
July 4, 1873

Most paraphrastical Sir:-

1   In my predecessive lexiphanic communication, I
2 gave you a compendious biographical sketch of Fritz, and
3 his amatorial experience. I now, rathe on this, our national
4 ferial occasion, again bring into requisition, my scaturient
5 pen, and plethoric cornucopia of arcane sesquipedalities,
6 and essay to excogitate yet another euphuistic, cabalistical
7 epistolary effusion; but, being at present, otherwise
8 somewhat pragmatically engaged, I shall be, necessarily,
9 more laconic.
10   On a certain dominical day, recently, I repaired to a
11 locality where audition was to be given to a certain
12 ecclesiastic. The conflux was ample.
13   The precentor, or accentor, of the quiristers,
14 inchoated the initial sonata with too much altitude of
15 intonation, which produced considerable raucity in his
16 guttural orifice before its termination; especially during the
17 antiphone.
18   Subsequent to this cantation, there was a general
19 taciturnity. This was broken by the orison of the boanergian
20 concionator. He was auricomous, and his countenance was
21 saturnine. His aspect was juvenile; his corporeal structure
22 was gracile; his nasal protrusion, or olfactor, possessed
23 singular tenuity, and cacuminated astoundingly. His theme
24 was esperance. In his exordial, or catastasis, he was
25 somewhat tranquil, but not didascalic. In a brevity of time,
26 however, he became stentorophonic and spumous at his

chief city of the west

giving author's meaning in plain language

1 former
2 pedantic   brief life sketch
3 love   early
4 holiday   demand   overflowing full
5 puffed up horn of plenty,difficult to understand,long words
6 try   think out   bombastic   mystical
7 letter outpouring
8 busily
9 brief
10 Sunday
11 a hearing
12 preacher   congregation   large
13 chief singer   leader of the choir
14 began   opening song   too high
15 musical tone   hoarseness
16 throat opening   close
17 responses
18 singing
19 silence   prayer   noisy
20 preacher   yellow or red headed
21 very grave   appearance   youthful   form
22 slender   nose   smeller
23 thinness   came to a point surprisingly   subject
24 hope   introductory   statement of heads of discourse
25 instructive
26 very loud in speaking   foaming

1 oral aperture. His sputations became frequent, and his
2 palpebral and ciliary organs gained indescribable celerity.
3 His chironomy was violent, and agonistic. Obstupefaction
4 seized his sectators in view of his supposed polymathy; but
5 his hermeneutical eclaircissement of his subject was
6 cryptic, acataleptic, and hypothetical, as well as
7 problematical and amphibological.
8   His ambilogy, antiloquence, and largiloquence,
9 exsuscitated my irrision. The eristical part of his homily
10 was fraught with alogies and paralogies, and furnished an
11 indubitable apodixis of his insipience in honorable
12 polemics, and homiletics. Towards dissentients, he evinced
13 such discourtesy and displacency as exacerbated my
14 interior nature.
15   When his course was zetetic, he propounded the
16 most amphigorical and extraneous interrogations; and his
17 responsions thereto were chimerical, catachrestical, and
18 totally irrelevant. In his vociferations, there was
19 occasionally a subitaneous disphony; seldom euphony, but
20 the must cruciating cacophony. As to his supernal
21 entheasm, he labored under a Muggletonian hallucination
22 altogether.
23   His sermocination had already transcended
24 compendiosity, and yet, he appended a platitudinous
25 peroration, in which he primarily inveighed against
26 pyrrhonism that is becoming so temerarious in this age; and
27 after frowning it down by the torvity of his visage, he
28 entered upon an inconcinnous, and very aristarchian
29 allocution to his sectators, in which he exprobrated their
30 attrition and their want of contrition, and genuflection in
31 their obtestations; and trenchantly, in very comminatory
32 terms, vituperated their stultiloquence, adiaphorism, and
33 their mutual obtrectations; and by protracted tautophonies
34 insisted on an auxesis of their foy, and an expurgation of
35 their nefarious piacularities and nefandous abominations;
36 by indesinent invocation. He depainted their multiform

1 mouth   spitting
2 eyebrows   eyelashes   quickness of movement
3 gestures   strained   astonishment
4 followers   great learning
5 explanatory interpretation
6 hidden   incomprehensible   not proven
7 questionable   doubtful
8 double meaning   lofty   boastful speaking
9 aroused   ridicule   conversational   sermon
10 filled   absurdities   false reasonings
11 undoubted proof   ignorance
12 debate   art of preaching   differers in belief
13 displeasure   irritated
14
15 inquiring   proposed
16 nonsensical   foreign   questions
17 replies   imaginary   far fetched
18 altogether inapplicable   shoutings
19 sudden discord   harmony
20 painful harshness   heavenly
21 inspiration   imaginary   mistaken inspiration
22
23 discourse   gone beyond
24 brevity   added   commonplace
25 exhortation   especially   spoke against
26 skepticism   headstrong
27 austerity   countenance
28 discourteous   severely critical
29 address   followers   chided
30 sorrow for sin only for fear of punishment,true repentance,
31 kneeling in prayer   entreaties   severely   threatening,
32 censured   follies   religious indifference
33 slandering   repetitions
34 increase   faith   cleansing
35 atrocious crimes   heinous   villainies
36 unceasing prayer   various temptations

1 tentations, and gave them a calid hortation to the
2 exercitation of esperance during the allotment of their
3 sublunary vitality. The vaticinated that then, in their adition
4 to the supernal world, they should be inenarrably felicitous.
5   In his finale, he insisted on a collatitious operation
6 throughout the assemblage, for redemption of theomachists,
7 and the ethnics to the fruition of ethical and theological
8 cognoscence; and after the education of pelf from our
9 nummary receptacles, he prepared us, in a benedictory
10 orison, for regression to our domiciliary tenements.
11   On the succeeding matin, I set out for this
12 metropolitan emporium, or megalopolis of the hesperian
13 plateaus, where I now temporarily abide.
14   The matutine part of that day was characterized by
15 all phases that possess puissance to impart satiety to the
16 visual, auricular, and olfactory powers of our complex
17 constitution.
18   The reorient exortive solar luminary, in his
19 emanation, or exurgence, from the oriental margaric
20 portals, cast luculent rayonant coruseations into the
21 innubilous azure concavity; and his effulgent candent
22 ascension coerced the subterrene seminal and radical
23 deposits to pelluate and diffuse vernal viridity over nature's
24 undulating surface. The sylvan regions, or rather, nemorous
25 and arbuscular riparian boscages, – were replete with the
26 most mellifluent canorous cantations of the pennated
27 tenants of the aerial regions. The herbaceous,
28 graminaceous, and floriferous foliage having been
29 humectated, and made rorifluent by nocturnal irrorations,
30 emitted the most grateful ambrosial redolence.
31   My functions are now emporetical, amanuensical,
32 and brachygraphical. I am quite negotiously engaged, and
33 somewhat a lychnobite.
34   As a nolleity to abide here coerces me, and
35 moreover, since – *remudas de pasturage haze bizerros*
36 *gordos*, – I shall perhaps, during the autumnal season,

1 fervent exhortation
2 exercise   hope
3 life beneath the moon   prophesized   entrance
4 celestial   indescribably happy
5 wind up   contribution
6 those who resist divine will
7 heathen   enjoyment   moral   divine knowledge
8 drawing forth   cash
9 money purses   closing prayer
10 return   homes [and vivers]
11 following morning
12 chief commercial city   western plains
13 for a time
14 early morning
15 appearances   power   satisfaction
16 seeing   hearing   smelling
17
18 returning   rising sun
19 coming forth   rising   eastern   pearly gates
20 brilliant   beaming   sparks
21 cloudless blue sky   bright   glowing
22 rising   forced   underground   seed root   plantings
23 sprout   scatter   springtime verdure
24 wavy   forests   groves
25 thickets   hedges   filled
26 sweet musical songs   feathered occupants
27 air   herbs
28 grass   flowers
29 moistened   dripping with dew   dews of the night
30 exhaled   delightful fragrance
31 occupation   mercantile   writing from dictation
32 stenographical   very busily
33 one who works at night and sleeps in the day
34 unwillingness   impels
35 [Sp.] change of pasture makes fat calves

1 resume my multivagous and mundivagant pererrations;
2 which may eventuate in my transfretation of the Pacific
3 ocean, and circumnavigation of this terrene.
4   Till which time,
5   I shall remain,
6   Your conterraneous cotemporary,
7   Ivan
8
9   "La critique est aisee, et l'art est difficle."

1 much and world over travels
2 result   crossing over
3 sailing around   earth
4
5
6 of same country   living at the same time
7
8
9 "Criticism is easy, but art is difficult."

Endnotes

1   This was Seneker's spelling, as opposed to sparsely. I don't know if that was intentional or an error.
2   This was Seneker's spelling, as opposed to chequered. I don't know if that was intentional or an error.
3   The original text had some sort of mark between "bonity" and "xenodochy", so I've elected to use a hyphen. I'm not sure if the intent was to concatenate the two words into one, or whether an additional letter was intended in that location.
4   The word subsequent didn't actually appear in the text here. There was a white-out space with no word present, and the word subsequent appeared on the right-side page in brackets.
5   This was Seneker's spelling, as opposed to demarcation. I don't know if that was intentional or an error.
6   The original text had an additional word included here "or ...". This was whited-out and is unreadable.
7   I'm not sure why, but Seneker hyphenated this word in the original text.
8   Seneker used this spelling in the original text. Webster's dictionary gives this as a variant spelling of the word Broncos.
9   Seneker did not provide any synonyms for cates, juncates, simnels, or succates. I have therefore provided dainty or choice foods for cates and crisp breads for simnels. Juncates seems to be similar to cates, and I was not able to find a synonym for succates.
10 This was Seneker's spelling, rather than multitudinous. I don't know if that was intentional or an error.

Appendix

I have not attempted extensive research to find mentions of Mr. Seneker in eastern Tennessee newspapers of his day. However, my relatives in Tennessee were able to provide a copy of the book *Adventures in Education, Sullivan County, 1773-1983,* by Thelma Gray Barnes (Sullivan County Retired Teachers' Association, 1985). This text has numerous mentions of Mr. Seneker, so I will excerpt those here.

Notably, *Adventures* begins with two quotations, one of which is from 'Superintendent J.E.L. Seneker':

> "True learning is that which takes hold of the child, awakens him to thought and action, and causes him to depend on himself."

The majority of the text of *Adventures* is an historical catalog of the schools and superintendents in Sullivan County, Tennessee. In describing the Walnut Grove School, *Adventures* notes "When Superintendent Seneker visited the school, he was surprised that he found no walnuts and no grove there. He said that Miss Mollie Hicks was teaching a good school."

His description as superintendent is one of the longer in the book, in part because of the length of his tenure being 22 years. Here is the bulk of the section on Mr. Seneker:

> J.E.L. Seneker (1893-1915) was born in Sullivan County 13 May 1848. He received his education at Jefferson Academy, Blountville, Tennessee and at King College, Bristol, Tennessee. He traveled extensively throughout the United States, Mexico, Alaska, and the north

Pacific. He learned to speak several languages fluently and taught school in Canada, in Hawkins County, and in Greene County. The Sullivan County Court elected him Superintendent of Schools in 1893, and he was subsequently re-elected every two years until 1915.

One of Superintendent Seneker's goals was to see that all teachers were properly licensed. He found that some had received certificates after taking only the reading examination. Tests were supposed to be given in spelling, writing, arithmetic, reading, history, geography, and subjects, such as algebra, Latin, chemistry, English literature, and others, depending on the subjects taught. When he had a shortage of teachers, he sought emergency certificates for teachers to fill vacancies. During summer, state and county normals were held and examinations were given to those who wished certificates to teach. College graduates were exempt from taking tests. Cost of the normal was one dollar and twenty-five cents ($1.25) per week and the same amount for a certificate.

A Sullivan County Teacher's Association was organized in 1893 for all educators and all friends of education. The meetings were held semiannually and many parents attended. Due to the size of the county and the problem of transportation, meetings were held in the three sections of the county: eastern, middle and western.

In 1907, Superintendent Seneker declared that progress must be made toward consolidation. This would bring a need for transportation and for this a good system of roads would be a necessity. The tax rate was too low for needed improvements. Sullivan, with a rate of one-fifty, had the lowest tax rate in the state. No other county had a tax rate under two dollars. Another need was for a guaranteed term of at least six months of school in order that better teachers would be willing to teach instead of choosing occupations with greater length of annual employment. Overcrowding and understaffing plagued the schools. According to the number of students listed for each school district, each teacher would have had from forty to sixty students. Some buildings were in serious need of repair while others should have been replaced. The county supplied a small portion of the building costs. The patrons donated materials and labor for the major portion of the building expense.

In July 1908, W.D. Lyon suggested that the Sullivan County Teachers' Association sponsor an educational column in his paper, *The Sullivan County Developer,* printed in Bluff City. This offer was accepted and Professor J. Craft Akard was chosen as editor-in-chief of the column. Superintendent Seneker wrote some of the articles, telling of his visits to each school. He gave his opinion of the condition of the building, the merits of the teacher, and the educational process in various schools, as well as the condition of the roads and the cooperation of the patrons. He was keenly perceptive of the factors contributing to public education at that time.

Superintendent Seneker issued a handbook to acquaint the teachers with all the schools of the county, to give the recommended course of

113

study from the first to the eighth grade, and to pass out other valuable information. He distributed four hundred copies in hopes that every teacher and every family in the county would become familiar with the school system in order to better judge it, its demands and needs. He also developed a point system for grading schools:

> School graded, 5 points; library and bookcase, 10 points; house painted and repaired, 18 points; flag, 2 points; individual drinking cups and cooler, 4 points; globes, maps, blackboards, and erasers, 2 points; oiled floors and two outhouses, 10 points; two good pictures framed, 2 points; proper seating and ventilation, 10 points; improvement organization maintained, 5 points; attendance at teachers' meetings, 1 point; visiting every pupil's home, 6 points; supervision of playground and games, 4 points; neat appearance of teacher, pupils, school grounds and room, 4 points; orderly assembling and dissembling, 1 point; flowers, 1 point; school fair, 8 points.

Superintendent Seneker served during a period of transition in public education from the old "hands off" policy exemplified by the state with its indifference to education, as shown by the first state Constitution, to a public awareness of the needs of an adequate system of public instruction. Prior to 1907, schools in each school district were controlled by three elected district directors. This made county wide uniformity difficult in the selection of teachers, purchase of supplies, and adoption of textbooks. After the establishment of the Board of Education, Superintendent Seneker hoped to motivate the voters with his newspaper column to seek improved school facilities through their elected officials. He emphasized that he had no voice in the disbursement of funds since the superintendent served only as secretary of the Board of Education.

In the early 1900s, the schools were branching out in extra-curricular activities for students such as the Boys' Corn Club. Superintendent Seneker, teachers, parents and boys met to organize the Boys' Corn Club. C.F. Striplin of farm demonstration work of the federal government and T.B. Thackston, land and industrial agent of the Southern Railway were present to make Sullivan County the leading corn producing county in East Tennessee. There were to be county, state and federal prizes, and exhibitions at the state fair.

During Seneker's term as superintendent, three new schools were built: Sullivan, near what is now Warrior Park; Flint Hill, near Easley in the vicinity of Bays Mountain; and Avoca, an up-to-date building costing several thousand dollars with the county contributing $1,000. Other schools were replaced by new structures, such as Cold Spring where the county paid $1,500 on a $6,000 building. He declared that during his superintendency, the old log schools had been torn away and replaced with modern frame buildings; the old slab benches had disappeared and students now sat in comfortable desks; new blackboards and teachers' desks added interest, beauty and efficiency to the classroom. A number of schools had purchased libraries.

Superintendent Seneker saw the administration of schools pass from school directors in seventy-three districts in Sullivan County to a board of education with seven members elected on a county wide basis. In 1907, the Tennessee Legislature discontinued the policy of school directors and established the board of education, to work with the superintendent, as the guiding force for schools. The school board contributed money and had authority in the establishment of public schools. Prior to this, schools were built by private citizens or by communities when and where they saw a need for a school.

Further, in the chapter titled "Pioneer Educators", the following is provided:

J.E.L. Seneker, superintendent for twenty-two years, served during the transition period from the one-room community school to the beginning of education operated by a county board of education. He began his superintendency with the observation that education was segmented with too many schools and too little supervision by teachers and superintendent, since the schools were operated by community school boards composed of school directors elected by each school district. Superintendent Seneker declared that the greatest need of the schools was for a "school wagon" to carry children to consolidated schools in wisely chosen locations. He was concerned that school directors, not the superintendent, had control of the expenditure of school funds. This problem improved with the election of a county board of education to cooperate with the superintendent on decisions involving school funds. Public support for schools was improved through a special column in the local papers which gave information on both accomplishments and needs of the schools. A teachers' association was organized and patrons of the schools were encouraged to attend the teachers' meetings.

Made in the USA
Las Vegas, NV
10 June 2022